STUDIES IN MARITIME ECONOMICS

STUDIES IN MARITIME ECONOMICS

R. O. GOSS

CAMBRIDGE
AT THE UNIVERSITY PRESS
1968

Published by the Syndics of the Cambridge University Press
Bentley House, 200 Euston Road, London, N.W.1
American Branch: 32 East 57th Street, New York, N.Y.10022

Standard Book Number: 521 07329 4

Printed in Great Britain
at the University Printing House, Cambridge
(Brooke Crutchley, University Printer)

CONTENTS

PREFACE

This book is a collection of papers, with the general theme of efficiency in sea transport, produced during the last few years, mostly whilst I have been acting as economic consultant on shipping to the British government. With the exception of this preface and the introduction they have all been published before. But, since they have appeared in four different journals, each with a rather specialized and largely separate audience, it seems appropriate to bring them together between the same covers.

This may, I think, be the more useful since the volume of work published by economists on this subject is rather small; and it is surprising that Britain, which has been by any standards a great maritime power for a very long time, should have produced no school of writers on the economics of sea transport. Indeed, until very recently the principal works in this field have all been foreign (though fortunately available in English—if sometimes only by way of a rather tortured translation). Professor S. G. Sturmey's *British shipping and world competition*,[1] Miss Carleen O'Loughlin's *The economics of sea transport*[2] and the historical works of Professor F. E. Hyde[3] have recently modified this situation but it remains to be seen whether this welcome trend will continue. Matters are not helped by the lack of economic statistics on shipping (a contrast with the mass of physical statistics e.g. in terms of gross tons—a non-homogeneous unit if ever I saw one): we have no reliable time-series on costs, revenue per ton of cargo on various routes, value added, tonnages of cargo carried by different types of ship, turnround, productivity, numbers of workers employed or their earnings. Nor, as yet, do we have any broadly-based index-numbers of cargo-liner freight rates or of that large and expanding trade carried by specialized bulk carriers and tankers on long-term charters or other contracts. Even the better-known indexes of tramp rates have recently suffered all the disadvant-

[1] Athlone Press (London, 1963). [2] Pergamon Press (London, 1967).
[3] *Blue Funnel* (University of Liverpool Press, 1957) and *Shipping enterprise and management 1830–1939—Harrisons of Liverpool* (University of Liverpool Press, 1967).

ages of being based-weighted in a period when technological advance, and thus substitution effects, have been large. They therefore systematically overstate rises and understate falls.

When re-printing essays of this nature it is tempting to take advantage of the opportunity to adjust the text here and there so as to improve the style, polish the arguments and disguise the errors. I am no less affected by *l'esprit de l'escalier* than the next man but in this work I have compromised with temptation by leaving the text virtually unaltered and collecting any comments and afterthoughts in a separate introduction. The references to papers 4 and 5 have been recast as footnotes.

The numerous friends and colleagues who have read, commented on and suggested improvements to these essays are all thanked in early footnotes to the papers concerned. But it is appropriate, here, to say that my gratitude to these people is not perfunctory; without their help and their patience in receiving, in some instances, draft after draft, these essays would probably never have been completed; they would certainly have done less justice to their subjects. I am, however, solely responsible for the views expressed and for any errors and omissions. Since I am a civil servant it is also appropriate to say that the views expressed are not necessarily those of the British government.

Finally, I am grateful to my wife and family for their forebearance in allowing me to work on these papers at weekends and on holiday, when they might justifiably have demanded more of my attention.

NOTE. Acknowledgements are due to the *Journal of Industrial Economics*, the *Journal of Transport Economics and Policy*, the Royal Institution of International Affairs and the Royal Institution of Naval Architects for permission to reprint the papers contained in this book.

INTRODUCTION

What really interests me is the cost of sea transport and how to get it down. (The *price* of sea transport—e.g. the freight rate—is another matter but if shipping is, in general, competitive then reductions in cost will necessarily be passed on to the consumer.) Consequently these essays have efficiency in sea transport as their general theme and this embraces seaports and the activities of ships in seaports as well as the ships themselves (hence the title, *Maritime economics*). As far as possible I have attempted not only to define and to describe some of the principal problems of this field of study but also to measure them. The more I have attempted to do this last the more I have been convinced that, in spite of all suggestions that the variability of costs is such that no set of costs can be fully representative, the results of actually doing the sums can be so useful that no reasonable doubts on the reliability of the basic data can invalidate the general conclusions.

We commence with what might be termed the 'political economy' of shipping in *The regulation of international sea transport*. This was commissioned by the Royal Institution of International Affairs as the first of two papers on the regulation of international transport; the second, by Mr T. L. Higgins, M.P., was on air transport and appeared in the November 1965 issue of *The world today*. The paper is a general survey of sea transport as it is, or might be, affected by such regulations as exist or seem likely to be considered in the future. It was, perhaps, inadequate in not dealing with container services which, since they are likely to be operated on a larger scale and to entail much larger entry costs, pose somewhat different questions. Necessarily, much of this paper was concerned with factual description; the treatment of the standard argument used in favour of shipping conferences (that without them we would have chaos) is possibly the most useful analytical part for the reader who is already familiar with the outlines of the subject. For this reprinting the quotation from Professor Sturmey has been given in full.

It is in fact high time that a serious study of shipping conferences was carried out by a competent economist free from pre-conceived ideas and who cannot be swept aside as a mere apologist, as a public relations man or as any other sort of interested party. It is, therefore, extremely fortunate that the Department of Applied Economics at Cambridge has started just such a study under the direction of Mr W. B. Reddaway, their Director of Research, financed by the Social Science Research Council and with the complete co-operation of two large groups of shipping companies. It can no longer be said (if it was ever true at all) that there are many in the shipping industry to whom economists equal critics, criticism means adverse criticism and adverse criticism is regarded as necessarily ignorant and wrong-headed. We must all look forward to the publication of this work with the greatest interest.

The second paper—*USA legislation and the foreign shipowner: a critique*—takes the long, complex and unhappy story of the American attempts to regulate cargo liner services to and from the USA up to April 1963. Since then the arguments have become even more complicated as rules and regulations (frequently of doubtful validity in international law and in terms of the comity of nations) have been promulgated by the Federal Maritime Commission, but much of what is described is still in force today. The Bonner Act (Public Law 87–346 of 1961) has neither been amended nor repealed and there is, as yet, no end in sight to this running sore between nations who in other fields are friends and allies. It is, however, just conceivable that the advent, on more important trade routes, of door-to-door container or other unitized services may change the pattern since regulation inside the USA is the concern, not of the Federal Maritime Commission (FMC), but of the Inter-State Commerce Commission and some co-ordination will be needed; presumably by the new Department of Transportation. This is, therefore, an opportunity to introduce new and more sensible rules. But, unless the Americans can be convinced (which so far they are not) of their folly in trying detailed regulation then the opportunity may be missed; indeed, the situation could become even worse.

And even if this opportunity were taken and the results were as sensible as most maritime nations would hope, there would still remain the minor trade routes on which specialized container-ships are unlikely to achieve the combination of considerable ship size, high load factor and frequent service which would enable them to compete effectively with conventional cargo liners and still cover the extra costs of the containers, the specialized berths and the cargo-handling gear needed ashore. More or less conventional cargo liners (possibly with engines aft, and with twin or treble—side-by-side—hatches) and probably offering discounts for palletized goods will probably remain on these trade routes for many years to come.

Since this paper was written a serious defence of the American position has appeared.[1] Mr May (who was formerly Managing Director of the Federal Maritime Commission and published this paper on his departure) makes some interesting points. First, he admits the inescapable nature of conflict (footnote, p. 794) between national jurisdictions. Secondly, he argues that the USA has legal jurisdiction over acts which take place elsewhere, even between citizens of other countries if these acts have 'substantial effects' on the USA. Since he goes on to talk of the domino effect of almost any trading action anywhere in the world upon everybody else's trade (p. 812) it is by no means clear where all this is supposed to end. Currently, for example, the FMC claims the right to regulate contracts made in the UK between a UK shipper and a UK shipowner and, naturally enough, the British government denies this right as constituting an infringement of British sovereignty. Thirdly, Mr May says (p. 850): 'World shipping can survive, even prosper, with one Federal Maritime Commission. It would be strangled if there were fifty.' As the late Mr Taft said of the slogan 'Trade: not aid', I like the second part.

The third essay—*Investment in shipping and the balance of payments: a case-study in import substitution policy*—is more or less self-explanatory and attempts to blow some of the cobwebs out of the thinking of many policy-makers who ought to know better. It is interesting that Sir Errington Keville made much the same points (though much more succinctly) in his speech[2] to the first meeting of the United Nations Conference on Trade and Development

[1] T. J. May: 'The status of Federal Maritime Commission shipping regulation under principles of international law', *Georgetown Law Journal*, Spring 1966.
[2] Reprinted in the *Annual Report* of the Chamber of Shipping of the United Kingdom 1964/5, pp. 229–30.

(UNCTAD). He was speaking in his capacity as Chairman of the International Chamber of Shipping, and since this includes the ship-owners' associations of Australia, Belgium, Canada, Denmark, Finland, France, Federal Republic of Germany, Greece, India, Italy, Japan, the Netherlands, New Zealand, Norway, Spain, Sweden, Switzerland, UK and USA, it seems that the argument commands widespread support even though one suspects that not every one of his constituents entirely agreed with him. The distinguished shipping economist Mr John Seland of Norges Rederforbund (the Norwegian Shipowners' Association) also expressed similar ideas to the Baltic and International Maritime Conference recently;[1] and so did Dr Alex Hunter of the Research School of Social Sciences, Australian National University, to the Melbourne Chamber of Commerce Forum on 'The shipping challenge'.[2] It seems, in fact, that there is widespread agreement among most of those who have studied the subject properly that shipping activities, as such, have no special effects on the balance of payments as compared with other uses of the same resources. Indeed, Sir Errington Keville went further in saying that 'the net effect (of investment in shipping on a nation's balance of payments) is usually negligible'.

The fourth paper—*Economic criteria for optimal ship designs*—was written at the suggestion of my friend and colleague (then in the Ministry of Transport; now in the Ministry of Technology) Mr Amos Sutcliffe, who was then Director of Merchant Shipbuilding and Repair. Mr Sutcliffe is a naval architect and he remarked to me that it was not enough for naval architects to be engaged on optimizing various parts of ships (such as the underwater hull form or the pro-peller) separately from one another and usually in purely physical terms. He suggested that we needed a method for optimizing the ship design as a whole and I could only agree. An optimal ship is, of course, the one which best serves the purpose for which it is intended; and since most ships (and all merchant ships) are intended to serve

[1] In a paper entitled 'Shipping in the balance of payments' delivered at Oslo, 5 June 1967, reprinted in *Scandinavian Shipping Gazette*, July 1967 and *Norwegian Shipping News*, July 1967.
[2] In a paper entitled *The economics of an overseas shipping line in Australia*; reprinted as 'Some notes on national shipping lines: The Australian Case', *The Economic Record*, March 1967.

economic purposes it follows that the process of optimization must be carried out in economic terms. With the vast majority of ships all that is needed is the application of the (by now) well-known discounted cash flow technique. When I examined the literature of naval architecture it became obvious that, insofar as the subject of ship optimization had been dealt with at all (usually in connection with aspects of hydro-dynamic resistance and powering), it had been without mentioning this particular technique and with what seemed to be an undue concentration upon fallacious methods such as those involving the maximization of the internal rate of return or—worse— the capital recovery factor.[1] Taxes, tax allowances and so on were universally omitted. (Professor Harry Benford's work, cited in this paper, was an exception but he gave no very clear indication of what questions could best be answered by which methods.) With the exception of Professor Benford none of the naval architects concerned appeared to have read any economic literature and no economists appeared to have taken any detailed interest in the subject or to have applied proper techniques of investment appraisal.

There is, of course, nothing new in d.c.f. The internal rate of return has been known and used for centuries and the principle of maximizing net present value goes back at least to 1890.[2] With the exception of some criticisms of previous works there is, I believe, very little in this paper that is original. Its point lies in its context and its justification lies in the keen interest that naval architects have taken in it. By the time this work appears most of the techniques described in that paper will be taught in at least one British university course for budding naval architects.

The paper was criticized (see e.g. Professor Sturmey's contribution to the written discussion which follows the original publication of the paper) because it assumed a knowledge of the future, and in particular of freight rates, which does not necessarily exist and also because of the complexity of the calculations required. I suspect that this last point had far more to do with the unfamiliarity of the calculations

---

[1] The capital recovery factor is not a normal economic concept. It is the ratio, expressed as a percentage, of the allegedly constant excess of cash revenue over cash costs to the capital cost. It resembles the Tutin–Baker–Kent formula described in this paper and suffers from most of its disadvantages.

[2] A. Marshall: *Principles of economics* (Macmillan, London, 1890) covers it.

than with their complexity since naval architects commonly perform much more complicated ones; but the point has some validity. In addition I now feel that the paper overstates the case against the useful simplification of ignoring the incidence of surveys and assuming the net cash flow timestream to be flat. With the important exception of rising real crew costs (on which see the next paper) this assumption really makes very little difference to the results. Rising real crew costs can be turned into an equivalent flat timestream by reducing them to their present value, turning this into an equivalent annuity and adding that to the remainder of the cash costs. This greatly reduces the calculation time required.

These criticisms, and also a direct request from a British ship-owner, led to the fifth of these papers—*The economics of automation in British shipping*—in which the word automation was stretched to cover all forms of incremental investment, whether automatic or not and in which numerous short-cut techniques were introduced. The British taxation system had been drastically altered in the interval between these two papers and I therefore took the opportunity to restate the subject matter in terms of corporation tax, free depreciation and investment grants. In spite of the alleged complexity of this new system it is perfectly determinate (except that income tax now has to be omitted or dealt with quite separately) and readily reducible both to a series of short-cut factors, of which tables are supplied, and to a series of ready-reckoners in which the results of the earlier tables are combined on various sets of assumptions. The result of all this is that, at the cost of simplifying the questions, valid answers can be obtained without any d.c.f. calculations, complex or otherwise, and with no more than a minimal set of assumptions about the future. Such assumptions are implicit in this kind of decision-making any-way and it is always better to have them made explicit; this, indeed, is one of the advantages of d.c.f.

In the written discussion which followed the original publication of this paper it was criticized by Professor Benford for omitting the situation in which the shipowner has a limited amount of capital to invest and where, therefore, he ought to maximize the ratio of net present value to capital cost. I replied that, in a world in which (thanks to a loophole in GATT) shipowners find it increasingly easy to borrow funds on extremely favourable fixed-interest terms, this was an unlikely situation. The paper was also criticized by Dr I. L. Buxton (of the British Ship Research Association) on grounds of spurious accuracy. He was right and in this re-printing I have reduced the number of decimal places shown.

The sixth paper—*The turnround of cargo liners and its effect on sea transport costs*—introduces the subject of seaport facilities and operations for the first time in this series and uses a variant of the discounted cash flow technique to apply sensitivity analysis to the liner cost data given in the appendix to the third of these papers. The study shows, in some detail, the methods which can be used for this purpose and gives ranges of results covering sufficient likely combinations of round voyage distance and turnround times to permit easy interpolation. For this reprinting the graphs have been redrawn.

On reflection I think that this paper would have been more useful if the shadow prices had been presented more in terms of the cargo tonnages handled per gross port day than in terms of the proportion of total time that the ship spends in port. The former is (or should be) known to every port authority: the latter is known only to the shipowners concerned. However, this is a small point which can be overcome by using Tables 6.2 and 6.4 together.

It is, of course, always possible that the breakdown of the costs of a typical cargo liner employed on any particular trade route may differ from that employed in the paper; and this is especially so in respect of the proportion of total costs represented by the cash costs of loading and discharging cargo. But, since improvements in turnround times are (at least initially) just as much value to shipowners as to port authorities who need this information, it should not be impossible to make corrections where they are needed. An interesting new presentation of some of the results was published in the *Research and Technical Bulletin* of the National Ports Council, June 1967.

The seventh paper—*Towards an economic appraisal of port investments*—was again the result of conversing with Mr Sutcliffe. Accepting that we could now optimize the ship he asked if we could not find a way to optimize the entire system of which the ship was a part—i.e. the ports plus the ships. One would be inclined to add 'and hinterland' too but, important though this can be, and especially in countries without well-developed inland transport systems,[1] I felt that this would have widened too far the scope of what was already a long and rather difficult paper.

In a sense, however, the optimization of the sea transport system resolves itself into optimizing the port for, given the expected port conditions and the necessary time-lag, shipowners who act rationally can be expected to optimize their ships in terms of the port facilities that they expect to use. The problem is, therefore, one of investment appraisal in the ports. But the pricing system employed in most ports is, from the economic point of view, so peculiar that discounted cash flow methods will not usually lead to the right answer. Cost-benefit analysis is therefore needed and in rather a specialized form with difficulties all its own. Another answer, of course, is to reform the pricing system but this may well take so long that the question remains of how we should take our decisions in the meantime. Here, cost-benefit analysis can be of considerable use and if there are some remaining degrees of ambiguity the method outlined in this paper should at least ensure that the more flagrantly non-optimal proposals are not adopted.

The paper says nothing of the intangibles which cannot, by their nature, be fully incorporated into a mathematical analysis. In any particular scheme there might be provision for recreational facilities, afloat or ashore, or for parks on reclaimed land. Hull, for example, has a pleasant City garden built on a disused dock. Airports commonly accompany their advanced technologies with fine examples of modern architecture: too many seaports are ugly, with an air of decay, desolation and decrepitude. Lord Devlin[2] has commented upon the pitiable efforts of port employers to provide proper wash-

[1] Cf. Mr S. F. Klinghofer's two reports: *Preliminary survey of factors contributing to the level of freight rates in the seaborne trade of Africa and related matters: Part I, The West and Central African sub-regions* and *Part II, The East African sub-region* (*including Madagascar and the Mascarene Islands*), UNO Economic Commission for Africa, referenced E/CN.14/TRANS/27, which lay great emphasis on the importance of improving hinterland communications in these regions. Shipping and even port costs, though significant, are of relatively less importance.

[2] *Final Report of the Committee of Inquiry under the Rt Hon. Lord Devlin into certain matters concerning the Port Transport Industry* (Cmnd. 2734) (HMSO 1965).

ing facilities for their workers and many of his recommendations are being carried out in British ports. But why not clear away the dirt and the unidentified piles of rubbish so often seen in odd corners of certain seaports? Why not plant trees? Why not design seaports so as to be aesthetically pleasing?

This paper was delivered in a more specialized and summarized form as a contribution to a Symposium on Dredging organized by the Institution of Civil Engineers. Together with the discussion and my reply this will appear in their *Transactions* in due course.

What conclusions can be drawn from all this in terms of the general theme? All available evidence goes to show that, on the whole, the profits available in shipping are mediocre. Of course certain periods are exceptional but freight rate booms are likely to be shorter than in the past because the time needed to build ships has fallen markedly with the introduction of new and better shipbuilding techniques. There are also exceptions in respect of certain routes, owners and, particularly, in terms of the more advanced ship designs. In tankers and dry bulk carriers these are the largest ships; in cargo liners they are the designs which concentrate upon cheap and rapid cargo-handling, preferably with twin—or treble—hatches to reduce horizontal movement in the holds and 'tween decks and with advanced cargo-handling equipment. But the average profitability still appears to be pretty poor. Long-term reductions in the cost of sea transport cannot, therefore, be achieved by squeezing the profits of shipowners. If we did so then they would be much less likely to invest in new ships and to continue to provide the services that are needed. If we cannot squeeze profits we must squeeze costs, and the best way to define costs for this purpose is in terms of the 'shadow prices' employed in the papers on turnround and port investments. One way of squeezing costs lies in the development and adoption of new and improved techniques (i.e. improved in the sense of providing a greater net present value). Another way is by the discovery and adoption of the optimum ratios between the various factors of production (capital, labour, fuel and so on) employed and the optimum ratios are again indicated by that technique which shows the greatest net present value. These two are analytically different in that one envisages the development of new techniques and the other concerns the proper choice between an array of existing techniques.

In the tanker and dry bulk carrier field costs can best be reduced by using larger ships. The differences in costs resulting from differences in ship size are, however, extremely sensitive to route length; so, therefore, is the optimal ship size, and it is only on the longer trade routes that the economies of ship size can be fully exploited. On the shorter routes one might do better to concentrate on improving loading and discharging times.

But it is with cargo liners that turnround becomes of greatest importance and the results shown in the essay on this subject should be enough to convince anyone that costs (and thus freight rates) can be reduced very substantially by drastic improvements in ship turnround times. Any doubts as to whether this is practicable should be resolved partly by examining the experiences cited in that paper (particularly those of the late Mr MacGillivray) and partly by looking at what can be done by providing modern quays, sheds and connecting inland transport facilities. But, providing the inland transport systems can take it, a great deal can be done with minimal capital investments in the ports by instituting continuous or double shift working. This is particularly important for nations who are short of capital. Overtime, however, is a very different matter; much of the work involved in conventional cargo-handling is physically hard and at the end of the day the men may be too tired to maintain their output.

Some writers have maintained that the practice, common amongst shipping conferences, of quoting the same freight rates between whole ranges of ports inhibits port authorities from improving their facilities. Why, it is asked, should they reduce the cost of moving cargo through their own port if they must, willy-nilly, share the benefits with some other port which may have invested less, or nothing at all? Professor Sturmey has, in addition, argued[1] that the conferences' practice of charging freight rates which discriminate between commodities according to their cost and speed of handling, and to the demand for them, and not between ports is against the shipowners' interests as well as everyone else's.

[1] S. G. Sturmey: 'Economics and liner services', *Journal of Transport Economics and Policy*, May 1967.

There are, however, arguments to the contrary and of these the strongest seems to be that we do not hear very much about this point from those most affected—the port authorities whose investments are supposed to be inhibited, nor from the shippers and consignees who, between them, pay the freight rates. There is nothing to stop them complaining to the conferences concerned or entering into negotiations with them. Conferences frequently negotiate and are the more likely to do so when, as it is alleged, their members also stand to gain. Professor Sturmey's point, however plausible, is therefore lacking in supporting evidence.

There is, however, a great deal of evidence that there are pressures on shipowners and on conferences to maintain and extend this practice. These pressures come from shippers, from governments and from port authorities themselves and are apparently intended to reduce competition between shippers in different regions and countries. Thus, for example, East and West Pakistan frequently insist on having the same freight rates even though the distances and the port efficiencies may be different. Both would like to have the same freight rates as Ceylon.

Some parts of this may be defensible on grounds of regional policy, but it is doubtful whether this argument can be maintained for every instance. Those who do not like shipping conferences may sometimes say or imply that they are restrictive practices, and bad ones at that. But, however strong or weak their case may be, there is at least as much reason to regard the institution as one which reduces competition between the consumers of sea transport as there is to regard it primarily as a means of reducing competition between shipowners.

In the same paper Professor Sturmey attacks the idea that marginal costs equal cargo-handling costs, an argument used, as he says, by himself and almost every other writer on the subject. His attack is rather different, however, from that contained in the first of these essays: his argument now concerns the fact that loading and discharging cargo involves ships time. 'The ordinary cargo liner has some flexibility of operation...Once *any* flexibility is introduced... the marginal cost...is then the handling charges plus the cost of ship's time spent in handling it'. But this is not necessarily true either. Marginal cost is the change in total costs associated with a unit change in output *per unit time*. A voyage of variable length is not a unit time. There are three ways in which the tonnage of cargo carried by a ship on a given route can be increased: the first is that described by Professor Sturmey, of spending longer in port; this reduces the number of voyages completed during the year (there is still a rise in annual throughput because the ocean passage remains the same) and marginal costs are therefore higher than he suggests. The second is to load and discharge more cargo by working overtime or introducing shiftworking; this will call for overtime or shift premia and therefore a considerable increase in cargo-handling costs but there will be no change in the time spent in port nor, therefore, in the number of voyages completed in a year. The third is by increasing the sea speed so as to complete more voyages per year; since daily fuel consumptions tend to vary as the cube of the speed and the number of days spent at sea on a given route very inversely as the speed it follows that the fuel costs per year will vary as the square of the speed. There will also be an increased risk of engine breakdown. Moreover, if (but only if) the ship is loaded down to her load line and raising the speed means carrying more fuel then this would reduce the amount of cargo carried per voyage. Which of these three methods of raising output per unit time the shipowner actually employs will, presumably, depend on their relative magnitudes; but they all show sharply rising marginal costs. Professor Sturmey is, therefore, correct in asserting that marginal costs are higher than he formerly thought but he is still understating them quite seriously. But in terms of the general theme of this work and of the efficiency of sea transport this point is not very important.

1

THE REGULATION OF INTERNATIONAL
SEA TRANSPORT

In 1963 (the latest year for which statistics are available) 1,330 million metric tons of cargo were carried in international seaborne trade—620 million tons of dry cargo and 710 million tons of oil. Since 1956 dry cargo has been growing at an average rate of $3\frac{1}{2}$ % per annum (though with year-to-year fluctuations ranging from -6 % to $+10$ %) and oil has been growing, more steadily, at an average rate of 9 % per annum.[1]

Of the 620 million tons of dry cargo, at least half can be identified as cargoes usually carried in bulk (e.g. iron ore, coal, and grain) by specialized bulk carriers or tramp ships which, like tankers, may be owned by the shippers of the cargo or (more often) chartered by them either for the voyage in question or for short or long periods of time. Some long-term time-charters extend for as much as twenty years, which is roughly the ship's life. Such ships generally carry near-homogeneous cargoes for one shipper at a time and, except when on long-term time-charters, move from trade to trade in accordance with variations in supply and demand. Apart from certain governments' regulations intended to confine some of their foreign (and often the whole of their coastal) trade to ships of their own flag (Professor Sturmey has estimated the extent of this flag discrimination as being of the order of 5 % of total international seaborne trade)[2] and intra-Communist-bloc services, such trades are open to all comers; there are no governmental or institutional restrictions on freight rates or carryings. Possible, but currently unimportant, exceptions to this have existed in shipowners' attempts to stabilize some open-market freight rates during periods of depression by encouraging some owners to lay their ships up, financing this through a levy on the ships that were still operating. As far as the post-war years are concerned,

[1] Statistics from *Maritime Transport, 1964*, OECD, Paris, 1965.
[2] S. G. Sturmey: *British shipping and world competition* (Athlone Press, London, 1962), chap. VIII.

[13]

the dry-cargo scheme failed to attract sufficient support to come into operation and the tanker scheme was supported by only half the eligible tonnage; it was virtually suspended in January 1965. The obvious difficulty with all such schemes is that any owner who continues to operate outside them can have all of the benefits and none of the costs.[1] On the other side of the coin, there have also been suggestions that charterers combine to reduce freight rates.[2]

Shipping conferences

But something rather less than half of international seaborne dry cargo is carried in liners,[3] most of which operate in shipping conferences. Basically, these are associations of shipowners and ship operators, often with permanent secretariats, in which freight rates are agreed. Usually (but not always) discounts are given to shippers who promise to confine all their shipments to members of the relevant conference. These discounts, which are commonly of the order of 5 to 15 %, may be given by contract and at once (the 'dual-rate system') or in respect of one period of loyalty at the conclusion of a second such period (the 'deferred-rebate system').[4] With either method the

[1] Cf. Shotaro Kojima: 'Shipping combinations as seen from the viewpoint of freight theory', *Kyoto University Economic Review*, July 1926. However, somewhat similar (though government-supported) schemes in the 1930s attracted nearly universal support, including support from the major oil companies.
[2] C. F. H. Cufley and British Sulphur Corporation Ltd: *Comprehensive summary and review of the world freight picture in 1962* (London, 1963), pp. 6–8. This work is a mine of facts on charter rates and carryings.
[3] *Ibid.*, p. 44, estimates liner carryings as 260 million tons in 1962, of which 250 million were in deep-sea trades.
[4] An extensive official literature on shipping conferences includes, from the U.K., *Shipping rings and deferred rebates*, Royal Commission Report, Comd. 4668, 1909, and various *Reports* of the Imperial Shipping Committee; from the U.S.A., *Investigation of shipping combinations* (four vols.), House of Reps. Committee on Merchant Marine and Fisheries (*Alexander Report*), 1913–14; *The ocean freight industry*, House of Reps. Anti-Trust Sub-Committee, 1962 (and many bound volumes of *Hearings*) (*Celler Report*) as well as the many volumes of *Hearings* of the House of Reps. Committee on Merchant Marine and Fisheries, 1959–61, leading up to the 1961 amendments of the US Shipping Act, 1916. A less extensive (but more useful) unofficial literature includes D. Marx, Jr: *International shipping cartels* (Princeton University Press, 1953); W. L. Grossman: *Ocean freight rates* (Cornell University Press, 1956); D. L. McLachlan: *Pricing in ocean transportation* (unpublished Ph.D. thesis) (Leeds, 1959); Sturmey, *British shipping*; and Ferguson *et al.*: *The economic value of the U.S. merchant marine* (Evanston, Ill., 1962) among the more important works.

shipper has the choice of, in effect, lower freight rates or freedom to ship as he pleases. To signatories of such agreements and non-signatories alike the liner operators guarantee stable freight rates, an adequate frequency of sailing and coverage of ports at each end of the trade, and ships which will sail on the advertized dates, full or not full. When they are unable to berth as many of their own ships as the volume of cargo requires they often charter ships (sometimes at a loss) in order to maintain adequate services. Alternatively, these circumstances will absolve the shippers from their contracts for the particular consignments concerned.

Numerous official investigations carried out in a variety of countries have produced reports having a number of points in common. In every case the investigators were obviously impressed by the evidence given, not only by shipowners but also by their customers, that shipping conferences were, in principle, necessary for the sensible conduct of business and that any disadvantages they might possess were more than outweighed by their advantages. Without them, it was frequently alleged, chaos would reign. Virtually all such investigations have concluded that, although conferences might have some undesirable practices (the commonest complaint was the non-publication of tariffs), they were good and ought to remain. This was also, broadly speaking, the conclusion of the 1964 UN Conference on Trade and Development, whose 'Common Measure of Understanding on Shipping Questions' states, *inter alia*: 'It was agreed that the liner conference system is necessary in order to secure stable rates and regular services.'

Indeed, most people concerned with the subject agree that if conferences did not exist the effects on freight rates and standards of service would be chaotic. There is, however, less agreement on why this chaos would occur. Academic writers[1] have attempted to explain it by basing their analyses on the fact that the only cost associated with the marginal ton of cargo is the coast of loading and discharging it; this averages some 25 to 30 % of the freight rate. Sturmey, for example, says:[2] 'Once a liner has been put on berth in a trade practically all costs become overhead costs and the additional cost of

[1] Notably D. Marx, Jr, D. L. McLachlan and S. G. Sturmey.
[2] *Op. cit.*, p. 323. He is following the sense of Marx and McLachlan.

carrying an extra ton of cargo is only the cost of loading and dis-charging that cargo. This means that if a liner operator can secure a rate of freight above the costs of handling the cargo, that makes a contribution to his overheads and, rather than sail with empty space, it is worth taking the extra cargo. Clearly, if all the cargo is at that rate the liner operator cannot survive, but so long as he is free to vary rates it will always pay him to accept such a rate rather than refuse cargo. With free competition, all rates would be forced to this level whenever any surplus of shipping space appeared and operations would become unprofitable for all concerned.'

But if rates were at such levels before the ship was committed to the berth then it would clearly be better to lay her up and thereby avoid all the costs of fuel, crew's wages, and so on. Are we to imagine that each ship would cut her rates to handling costs after she has been put on the berth? Such a practice would be profitable only if it was thought that she would otherwise sail part-empty. Estimates of this cannot usually be revised (for the pre-berthing estimate must have been different) during loading since, first, it is common to overbook cargo before and during loading,[1] and secondly, most of the cargo arrives only during the last few days of loading because shippers mistakenly believe that what goes in last must come out first. Finally, there is not the slightest historical evidence that anything like the process implied has ever happened.[2] If it were to happen more than a very few times it would give rise to a persistent expectation of such possibilities among shippers; no such expectation exists (even where there are non-conference operators), nor are there references to it in the trade press. There is, however, evidence that, without conferences, liner freight rates would be unremunerative and unstable; shippers and ship-owners are united in finding such a situation objectionable. The only doubt concerns the extent of this instability and the reasons for it.

The shippers tend, by and large, to support conferences because, in the first place, existing and recent liner rates are typically no more than 3 to 10 % of their f.o.b. prices and tend to average near the lower end of this range. No conceivable cut in rates can, therefore,

---

[1] Cf. R. B. Monteath: 'The effect of modern cargo handling methods on the design of ships and ports', *ICHCA Quarterly Journal*, October 1964, p. 16.

[2] See e.g. F. E. Hyde: *Blue Funnel* (University of Liverpool Press, 1957).

have very much effect either on their profits or on their volume of trade. Liner shippers typically dispatch their goods in consignments of no more than a few tons at a time (and conferences, with rare exceptions such as special projects and charters, apply the same rates to all shipments regardless of size and the aggregate business done with the shipper concerned, i.e. they do not discriminate between shippers of the same commodities); because of the economies of scale in ship size they cannot charter a ship on their own account without paying absurdly high rates per ton of cargo. In order, therefore, to be able to offer their goods for sale they must be assured of the existence of a frequent common-carrier type of service, preferably at predictable rates. This is precisely what the conferences offer. Shippers are further assisted because the knowledge of frequent services and stable rates enables them to minimize the costs of production and inventory control. The identity of views between shippers and shipowners is, therefore, not nearly as surprising as may appear at first sight.

Thus the shipping conference is not so much an anti-competitive device as a co-ordinating one. In some trades this co-ordination extends to the agreed spacing of sailings, the sharing of ports (in order to reduce duplication of sailings and competition for congested berths) and to the pooling of revenues (usually after deduction of certain costs, such as cargo-handling). Particular trades often demand certain specialized characteristics in ships; for example, shallow draft for the River Plate ports or the Bay of Bengal, refrigerated spaces for perishables, or large derricks for heavy lifts; and without the protection from some trading risks that shipping conferences provide shipowners would be less willing to provide any specialized characteristics or equipment in their ships. Moreover, they would also be less willing to build up the elaborate business organization necessary for the efficient conduct of a liner trade or to take any account, in their long-term decision-making, of the long-term needs of the trade they carry.

The level of freight rates (and thus of profits) in a conference is limited by the fact that, if they are raised too high, competition will be attracted from outsiders. Dual-rate contracts and deferred-rebate systems notwithstanding, it is quite impossible for any conference to insulate itself from the supply–demand position of world shipping; a conference may call itself 'open' (i.e. ready to accept new members prepared to operate on conference terms) or 'closed', but it can never prevent a determined shipowner from entering the trade and cutting rates (or offering secret rebates) until the conference is forced to accept him. Numerous examples of this exist in both pre- and post-war years and in both types of conference. Some of them reveal a weakness in the conference system: by concentrating on the shippers both dual-rate and deferred-rebate systems leave the consignees open to persuasion—and no shipper can ignore his consignee's instructions.

Liner shipowners do not resemble those monopolistic entre-preneurs, beloved of economics textbooks, who maximize short-run profits. If they did, and given the general inelasticity of demand for their services, then their freight rates would be several times higher than they are. Instead, they maximize profits only in the long run and, because any new operator who has once competed his way into a con-ference is likely to stay there indefinitely (thereby permanently reduc-ing the shares available for all the other members), they attempt to set their general level of freight-rates sufficiently high to allow them to make profits but not sufficiently high to attract fresh competition whether from newly built ships or from those originally built with some other trade (or no particular trade) in view. Unlike the air (and flag discrimination apart), the seas and the seaports are open to all and, as Sturmey has remarked,[1] competition in this industry comes in large increments or not at all. (Competition from air freight comes in small increments and is currently rather insignificant; however, it is growing rapidly and may well become important in the future. Shippers who use air freight suffer none of the penalties mentioned in connection with dual rates and deferred rebates.)

Not only is there implicit competition from potential liner opera-tors: there may also be explicit competition from tramp operators. Many tramp trades are unbalanced; that is to say, there is more cargo in one direction than in the other. To some extent this may be modi-fied by multilateral trading (e.g. returning from B to A by way of C, and possibly D, E etc.) but it is likely that some 'backhaul' or 'return load effect' will remain. If it does (as, for example on the

[1] S. G. Sturmey: *Some aspects of ocean liner economics* (Manchester Statistical Society, 1964), pp. 20–1.

North Atlantic shipping route, where total eastbound cargo movements, seaboard to seaboard, far exceed total westbound cargo movements) then, regardless of whether such a backhaul effect exists in
liner cargoes alone, there will be different competitive pressures and
therefore different freight rates in the two directions. Nor can it be
argued that dual-rate or deferred-rebate systems can isolate the conference from tramp competition; if the rates are too high then tramps
will undercut them sufficiently to make the loss of discounts or of
deferred rebates worth while to the shippers who use them. In the
extreme case, where there is a strong backhaul effect, tramp ships
faced with the choice of sailing in ballast or carrying cargo may opt
for the latter at any rates in excess of cargo-handling charges *minus*
the cost of buying, loading, and discharging ballast.

All this, however, concerns only the general level of rates. Within
any general level, a structure of rates has to be arranged and this does
not seem to be a problem susceptible to logical solution on any basis
of costs. Of course, differential cargo-handling costs can be, and are,
taken into account but the major part of the freight represents the
costs of ships' time (including capital charges). As Sturmey[1] says, this
is a problem in overhead allocation to which there is no 'right' solution. Answers may sometimes be found by precedents (which may be
out of date) or by 'charging what the traffic will bear' (or, more
accurately, by *not* charging what the traffic will *not* bear). In practice
this means that the cash costs (and the speed) of loading and discharging the commodity concerned, its weight and the space that it
may be expected to occupy, its value and freight rates of competing
forms of transport (tramps and other liner routes, including those
involving trans-shipment) are all taken into account. It is *always* in the
interests of the conference to set the rate so as to encourage the movement of cargo by its ships—never the reverse. However, it is perfectly
possible that, in a tariff possibly containing a few thousand items and
related to constantly changing conditions of trade, anomalies will
occur and adjustments will frequently need to be made. This is one of
the principal occupations of conference meetings and of their
secretariats.

[1] *Ibid.*, p. 2, footnote.

Negotiations between conference and customers

Because these questions of freight rates, sailing intervals or, indeed, anything else can constantly arise and may be important, it is desirable that there should be an intermittent, if not continuous, dialogue between the conference and its customers. This requires that there should be some organization of the shippers (and possibly of the consignees) which can represent them in negotiations. This was formally recognized by a meeting of ten European Ministers of Transport[1] in March 1963, when they stated, first, that they regarded the conference system as indispensable, and, secondly, that 'means should exist, and should be widely known to exist, of ensuring fair practices and discussing grievances that shippers or groups of shippers may have against conferences', adding that 'these means should preferably be provided by the conferences themselves rather than by governments'. The Ministers agreed to satisfy themselves that conferences of which their shipowners were members provided broadly similar machinery for the resolution of disputes between conference members (i.e. between shipowners), for the discussion of shippers' grievances and for providing some method (such as arbitration) for dealing with disagreements which could not be solved by the conference itself.

Further meetings were held in Paris and London in June and December 1963, respectively. At the latter, the Committee of European Shipowners (the original ten nations plus, since December 1963, Japan) presented a Memorandum which responded to these requests, and attached a Note of Understanding[2] which had been reached between European conference lines and European shippers (this term here includes both exporters and importers). Both parties noted with satisfaction the support that the Ministers had given to the conference system and agreed on the importance of establishing methods to ensure fair practices and facilities for the discussion not only of grievances between shippers and conferences but also of all matters of

---

[1] Belgium, Denmark, France, Federal Republic of Germany, Greece, Italy, Netherlands, Norway, Sweden, and United Kingdom.
[2] For text, see Chamber of Shipping of the UK *Annual Report* 1963–4, Appendix A. This brief summary cannot do justice to its full provisions.

mutual interest. There followed detailed proposals for regular meetings and providing for the reference of outstanding matters to the appropriate Shippers' Council by any shipper who failed to reach agreement with the conference directly. Where shipper/shipowner, shipper/conference, and Shippers' Council/conference discussions had all failed to produce agreement, there was provision for reference to an 'Independent Panel' to consist of three people nominated by shipowners and three nominated by Shippers' Councils, none of whom was to be directly concerned with the matter at issue. Such a panel could co-opt an independent chairman if it wished. Due regard was to be paid to all the interests concerned, whether directly represented or not. (Many countries do not yet have Shippers' Councils).

In practice there has so far been little use of these arrangements: Shippers' Councils can represent, and have represented, their members in negotiations with conferences but there has been no need for independent panels. In these negotiations the Shippers' Councils have been continuing a long tradition. Conferences have, in fact, always negotiated with their customers; their main difficulty in doing so has been the lack of shippers' organizations. In certain trades regular and detailed negotiations are conducted. In the New Zealand trades, for example, independent accountants have for many years had free access to the shipowners' books and have compiled annual aggregate statistics and cost accounts of the trade. To the total cash costs of operating the ships they add agreed allowances for overhead costs, the replacement of ships, and for a return on capital; this total is then compared with the aggregate revenue and the resulting excess or short-fall is then used as a basis for negotiating the general level of rates between the conference members concerned and the Producers' Boards of New Zealand who control most of that country's exports (other than wool). Some other trades (such as the Australian) have methods that are broadly similar and these arrangements are known as the 'formula system'.

But it would be wrong to imagine that the addition to shipowners' costs of a 'reasonable' level of profit led to a reduction in the general level of freight rates (the formula system does nothing about the relationships between rates on different commodities); and it would be equally wrong to think that shipowners found a way to a quiet, if only moderately profitable, life. For, on the one hand, the formula results have in most years (in the New Zealand trades and probably in others) shown 'formula deficits' and have thus provided justification for increasing the rates; and on the other hand, the world surplus of tonnage which followed the collapse of the 1953–7 shipping boom has meant that the potential competition from outside the conference (and, in many trades including the New Zealand one, actual competition at cut rates, with secret rebates to shippers and/or consignees) has meant that these rate increases have not been obtained. Formula or no formula, it remains impossible to insulate any one trade, or group of trades, from the general shipping situation.

The close relationship which exists in the New Zealand trades between a small number of shipowners and (apart from wool) a small number of shippers led, in 1962, to the joint appointment of a small independent committee with wide terms of reference to examine the whole subject and to recommend methods for improving matters. Their Report,[1] and their recommendations, form one of the most detailed and expert studies of a specific liner trade that has ever been carried out and may be regarded as a model for studies in other trades.

The US approach

This 'self-regulating' approach, however, contrasts strongly with that of the United States, the only country which has attempted the statutory regulation of liner conferences.[2] Many objections have been raised to these attempts (which started with the Shipping Act of 1916 and

---

[1] Producers Boards' Shipping Utilisation Committee, New Zealand, and New Zealand Trade Streamlining Committee, London: *New Zealand overseas trade: report on shipping, ports, transport and other services*, February 1964.

[2] For further details of US attempts to regulate liner shipping, see D. Marx, Jr: *op. cit.*; R. O. Goss: 'USA legislation and the foreign shipowner: A critique', *Journ. Indust. Econ.*, November 1963; and P. V. C. Sprigings: 'The effect of American legislation on liner conferences', *Journ. Instit. Transport*, March 1965. For an American lawyer's views (at variance with the last two), see: 'Rate regulation in ocean shipping', *Harvard Law Review*, January 1965 (no author given). Many other countries have, or appear to have, powers to control shipping conferences. See A. Frihagen: *Linjekonferanser og kartell-lovgivning* (Universitetsforlaget, Oslo, 1963). Only the USA has actually used such powers to any significant extent.

really became important with the amendments to that Act passed in 1961 and known as Public Law 87-346) and, in fact, practically every maritime nation in the world has lodged protests with the United States. It is argued that, in view of the success of self-regulation, statutory control is unnecessary. It is further argued that the ways in which the United States attempts to regulate liner shipping are actively harmful, in that they impede, delay, and raise the costs of the ordinary conduct of trade and that they create conflicts of jurisdiction with other countries. (There is, however, no argument over the necessity of a shipping statute in the United States, for the Anti-Trust Acts are of such wide scope that, if shipping were not to have exceptional provisions, conferences would be illegal *per se*.) The argument is concerned with the American position that, if conferences are to be legal, their basic agreements, their rates and all their actions, whether inside American jurisdiction or outside it, should be subject to regulation by the United States and *in the interests of the United States*. Indeed, the regulatory body, the Federal Maritime Commission (FMC), is specifically enjoined in the Act not to permit agreements 'detrimental to the commerce of the USA, contrary to the public interest or unjustly discriminatory or unfair...' and, although the exact meanings of these phrases are unclear (because none of them is defined), one is left in no doubt as to their general purport.

But international trade necessarily involves at least two countries and very often third countries as carriers. (British shipping earns well over 40 % of its freight from cargo carried between foreign countries.) Agreements, meetings, and correspondence concerned with any given trade may take place anywhere and the documents may be located anywhere. If they are outside the United States then that country has no jurisdiction; nor, if she claims such jurisdiction, has she any way of enforcing it. Amongst the effects of the US shipping legislation, therefore, has been the passing in several countries (of which the United Kingdom is one) of Acts prohibiting, or giving powers to prohibit, the supply of information concerning shipping activities to the FMC and to the US courts. The shipowners of these countries have been strongly supported by the shippers and their councils as well as by their governments.

There are, in fact, two ways of regulating international common-carrier services by sea: there can be self-regulation by agreement between shippers and shipowners (possibly with some gentle encouragement from their governments) or there can be internationally agreed regulation by governments. In view of the success of the former method, the latter would seem as superfluous as it would be difficult to achieve. What is clearly undesirable is regulation by one country only, acting solely with regard to its own national interest.

2

USA LEGISLATION AND THE FOREIGN SHIPOWNER: A CRITIQUE[1,2]

On 3 October 1961 there came into force in the USA an extensive series of amendments to the USA Shipping Act, 1916. These amendments, known as Public Law 87–346, were designed to make the regulation of seagoing common carrier services (cargo liners) more effective. This Act, in its amended form, is already having great effect on non-US shipowners as well as upon American ones and, unless repealed, is likely to have much greater effects in the future. It constitutes an important attempt at the statutory regulation of imperfect competition in the foreign-going shipping industry; an attempt made by one nation acting without the agreement, and in many cases against the protests, of the other nations concerned, whether they are concerned as importers, exporters or as carriers.

The original Act followed the 1914 report of the Alexander Committee[3] and to some extent exempts the industry from the operation of the Anti-Trust Acts. It specifically allows the formation of conferences to agree freight rates and inter-carrier agreements on other subjects, but prohibits the use of deferred loyalty rebates to retain patronage and the use of 'fighting ships' (ships specially berthed alongside a non-conference competitor's ship, operating at drastically reduced freight rates and financially supported by conference members).

The economic justification[4] of steamship conferences lies in a

[1] The principal source available on this subject in the UK are the bulletins of the Congressional Information Bureau (CIB) which have been extensively relied on in this article.

[2] Thanks are due to Mr L. K. Cooper, director of a leading British shipowning company, for help on several aspects of this article.

[3] House of Representatives Committee on Merchant Marine and Fisheries *Investigation of shipping combinations*, 62nd and 63rd Congress, Washington, DC, 1913–14, 4 vols.

[4] For a fuller discussion of this question see D. Marx, Jr: *International shipping cartels* (Princeton, 1953), and S. G. Sturmey: *British shipping and world competition* (London, 1963), chap. XIII.

[25]

combination of factors. The typical liner shipper wishes to ship frequently and in small consignments; because of the economies of scale in ship size (as distinct from fleet size), the ratio between the typical consignment and the typical vehicle may be anything from 1/500 to 1/2000. The shipper therefore demands a regular or at least a frequent service. At the same time there are tramp ships which are often in search of cargo. If they cannot get it they must ballast, which involves the ship's time spent loading and discharging the ballast, the cash cost of doing so (and of purchasing the ballast) as well as the voyage time. To the unfixed tramp-owner, therefore, the opportunity cost of lifting liner cargo is extremely low. The incidence of tramp vessels in this position is irregular and unpredictable, presenting risks to the potential liner operator which he is reluctant to bear without the existence of a conference able, by means of some effective tie, to preserve stable rates of freight and to deter shippers from making use of the tramp services. Such ties are found in the deferred loyalty rebate, the dual-rate contract and the fidelity commission (the last is a loyalty rebate which is not deferred). Unlike the first, the last two periodically allow a shipper to cut the tie without cost to himself—in other words to change his mind.

It may be objected that where there are fluctuations in demand the usual effect of stabilizing a price is to increase the fluctuations in the volume of trade and that this is hardly the way to secure economies. But this argument depends for its force upon the elasticity of supply. The elasticity of supply of liner services on any given route is, in practice, infinite up to the point where serious and chronic congestion exists in the terminal ports. Below this point liner operators are willing to charter ships from other routes, if necessary at a loss, to cover short-term fluctuations and in the long period they will, of course, build or buy new ships. Above this point they may, in the short period, place a surcharge on all freight rates. This is rather unusual and is employed more as a means of persuading reluctant port authorities into improving their facilities than as a means of covering high marginal costs. There appear to be no diseconomies of scale in the long period.

Conferences, whether open or nominally closed, are inhibited from raising their freight rates to the point where unusually large profits are being made because the trading 'rights' are regarded as one of their members' most valuable assets; and because any other shipowner might set up a service outside the conference when profits reach this level. Moreover, if he really wants to do so, any shipowner may fight his way into a conference, even one that is nominally closed; obviously, this will reduce the shares of all the existing members throughout the foreseeable future. In other words, conference members are generally in the usual position of long-run profit maximizers in that potential competition may be more important than actual competition.

Under section 15 of the Shipping Act, 1916, agreements between carriers were to be allowed only after approval by the government agency responsible for administering the Act. The title of this agency has varied from time to time; currently it is known as the Federal Maritime Commission (FMC). Until President Kennedy's Reorganization Plan No. 7 of 1961 came into force it was called the Federal Maritime Board (FMB) and was one of several government agencies which, in different fields, combined regulatory with promotional functions. The FMB was also responsible for administering the Merchant Marine Act of 1936, which provides for subsidies for capital and operating costs of US ships to levels supposed to be equivalent to those of their foreign competitors, research designed to increase efficiency and so forth. These regulatory and promotional functions of the FMB were clearly in conflict and it is hardly surprising that the Merchant Marine Act, 1936, gained far more attention than the regulatory Act. Since the reorganization plan came into effect these functions have been divided between the FMC and a new body called the Maritime Administration.

Throughout the consideration of USA shipping policies it must be remembered that there is a sharp conflict between the enforcement of the Anti-Trust Acts by the Department of Justice, which has the effect of keeping freight rates fluctuating and lower than they would otherwise have been, and the desire to minimize the burden on the American taxpayer of supporting the high-cost American merchant fleet by keeping freight rates stable and high. The former arouses strong feelings among many American legislators. The latter is rarely made explicit in Congressional hearings, although it clearly underlies much of the thinking on this subject [see, for example, the remark of Rep. Bonner, Dem., during the House Committee on Merchant Marine and Fisheries hearings on PL 87–346: 'I just do not feel that the Department of Justice realizes that we have a merchant marine and we are trying to find some way to maintain it on the high seas' (26 April 1961); a remarkably revealing comment, considering that PL 87–346 had to do only with monopoly control] especially in view of the growing opposition to these subsidies. [See, for example, an editorial in *Fortune*, October 1961, p. 104, headed 'Let's give shipping subsidies the deep six' (i.e. throw them overboard), arguing that as subsidies encourage inefficiency US shipowners should be allowed to reduce their costs by building ships abroad and recruiting foreign seamen at foreign wage-rates; also 'The economic value of the US merchant marine', Transportation Center, Northwestern University, Illinois, 1961, a lengthy study paid for by the Committee of (subsidized) American Steamship Lines (who were considerably surprised at the result), upon which the above editorial was largely based. It is also noteworthy that in 1962, when the reservation of the US coastwise trade to US flag (i.e. US built and manned ships) proved to have raised west coast/east coast lumber rates to four times the British Columbia/east coast USA level, the US Government reaction was not to introduce subsidies into the coastwise trade, but to allow foreign ships into the trade to bring rates down.] It is also worth remembering that the experience of the legislators, who drafted and redrafted PL 87–346 again and again whilst they were considering it, was confined to *promoting* the US merchant marine. Never before had they entered the field of international legislation, or even that of monopoly control.

The ostensible purpose of PL 87–346 was to legalize permanently the system of dual-rate contracts, as a tie between conferences and shippers. Under this system the conference tariff may cite two rates for any commodity: an ordinary rate and a lower rate applicable to shippers who sign contracts with all the conference members (conferences as such rarely have legal personality and cannot therefore enter into contracts themselves) promising to confine their shipments to conference vessels.

Until 1958, when the Supreme Court cast doubts on their legality,[1]

[1] The Japan-Atlantic Case, FMB *v*. Isbrantsen Co., 356 US 481 (1958).

dual-rate contracts had been widely employed by conferences trading to and from the USA. Indeed, almost everyone thought they were legal. After 1958 contracts already in existence were validated by hastily enacted legislation of limited duration, but renewed when necessary, pending full consideration of the question by Congress. This legislation, however, did not permit new contract systems to be established, nor existing ones extended; it simply froze the situation, rendering it increasingly difficult for conferences to adjust themselves to changing patterns of trade.

This full consideration was intended to be undertaken by the House Committee on Merchant Marine and Fisheries (the Bonner Committee), who produced the original drafts of PL 87–346, and the Senate Committee on Commerce. Meanwhile, however, the whole of the FMB's record in its regulatory function was being investigated by the House Anti-Trust Sub-Committee (Celler Committee). This committee found that the FMB staff were confused between their promotional and their regulatory functions and that the latter had been seriously neglected. Indeed, the section of their Report[1] dealing with this is subtitled 'A study in desultory regulation'.

These two committees each held lengthy hearings, at which there appeared witnesses representing foreign and US shipowners, shippers, foreign governments and various departments of the US Government. Generally, the shipowners recognized that statutory action was necessary, first in the continuance of the 1916 Act to exempt them from the Anti-Trust Acts and secondly to permit dual-rate contracts, but thought the regulation of their actions should be kept to a minimum, since, if it was not, problems of international jurisdiction and enforcement would arise; the shippers, both individuals and representative associations, supported the idea of conferences and said that if the shipowners wanted dual-rate contracts to be allowed they would support that too; the foreign governments objected to the potential infringement of their sovereignty in the bills under consideration and the US government departments each presented its own particular point of view.

Contrary to the practice in Britain, government departments in the USA appear to see no objections to presenting evidence in public

[1] Washington, DC 1 March 1962.

which diverges from that of other departments. Thus, the State Department emphasized the lack of authority for regulating the activities of foreign citizens outside the USA whether they were engaged in the foreign commerce of the USA or not; the Department of Justice emphasized the Anti-Trust aspects of the proposed legislation almost to the exclusion of other aspects; the FMB wanted more room for administrative determination and investigations (by itself) and the General Accounting Office wanted freedom to use the monopsonistic power of the US Government to get lower freight rates for itself.

Provisions of PL 87–346

The combined effect of these two committees, whose chairmen maintained close liaison, was that PL 87–346 did far more than legalize dual-rate contracts; it did legalize them (in a new section 14 (*b*)), but only under such restrictive conditions as considerably to reduce the tying effect.

Section 14 (*b*) begins, not by legalizing existing contract systems and authorizing their extension and establishment elsewhere, which was what the shipowners wanted, but by stating that the FMC, on application, was to permit those dual-rate contracts which were equally available to all shippers, not 'detrimental to the commerce of the USA, contrary to the public interest or unjustly discriminatory or unfair as between shippers, exporters, importers or ports, or between exporters from the US and their foreign competitors' and which also contained these provisions: contract cargo to go non-conference if no conference vessel available at reasonable notice; 90 days' notice to shippers of a rise in rates; only those goods to be included of which the contract shipper had the legal right to select the carrier (unless he deliberately diverted himself of this legal right); no diversion of cargo from natural routings not served by the conference where direct movement was available; damages for violation limited to actual (i.e. not penal) damages or contract freight less handling costs; the contract shipper to be able to withdraw on 90 days' notice; a spread between contract and non-contract rates which the FMC found to be reasonable and in any case not more than 15 %; most bulk cargoes to be excluded. Finally, the contracts were to include such other provisions as the FMC might require or permit.

Shipowners regarded these provisions as so hedging the right to establish effective dual-rate systems as to be almost worthless. Particularly onerous were the provisions that the carriers would be unable to enforce the contract on goods sold 'free on board' or 'free alongside ship' (f.o.b./f.a.s.) where the consignee, not the shipper, has the legal right to select the carrier; and the lack of any provision authorizing the cancellation of a contract violated by a shipper. In practice it is impossible for a shipowner to determine who has the legal right to select the carrier, and he has no access to the contract of sale to see whether it is on a cost, insurance, freight (c.i.f.) or a f.o.b./f.a.s. basis, while the limitation of damages to some equivalent of roughly a 50 % surcharge on the freight which would have been paid to the contracting carriers, if and when the carrier can prove the shipper has broken the contract, is claimed to be quite ineffective; also the impossibility of proving that a shipper divested himself of the legal right to select the carrier deliberately means that he can do so quite freely. Shipowners maintain that nothing less than the threat of cancelling the contract and thereby charging 10 or 15 % more on all his previous and subsequent shipments during the contract period will deter a shipper from occasionally supporting non-conference lines.

Following the provision of section 14 (*b*) that the contracts should contain such other provisions as the FMC might require or permit the FMC issued detailed draft rules[1] which were intended to govern the operations of dual-rate systems. These draft rules were not published until six months after enactment of PL 87–346. Shipowners protested strongly against the form and content of these proposed rules. Nine months later the FMC issued 'proposed final rules'[2] on the same subject. Shipowners again protested.

Without going into the details of these protests, which were numerous and lengthy, their essence was that any contract system established under the proposed rules would be quite ineffective at accomplishing its purpose, that of deterring the sporadic incursion of outside vessels. These protests were not based on ignorance of the

[1] Docket 983, Federal Register, 21 March 1962.
[2] Federal Register, 3 January 1963.

law, for every shipowner concerned with American trades has been compelled to become increasingly expert in the intricacies of the system simply in order to carry on his business. Moreover, these protests were made through and on the advice of American counsel specializing in this field, representing both US and foreign lines.

Meanwhile, a further provision of PL 87–346 had expired. This stated that dual-rate contracts legal (under the temporary legislation) immediately before its enactment should be amended to comply with the new Act within six months; whereupon they were to remain legal for another year. This period expired on 3 April 1963.

As noted above, during this time the FMC had neither produced rules acceptable to shipowners nor any which it was prepared to defend in the legal actions likely to follow a decision to enforce them without agreement. On 3 April 1963, therefore, President Kennedy had to sign yet another Act amending the Shipping Act of 1916, again extending the life of existing dual-rate contract systems for another year.

The upshot of all this is that the ostensible purpose of PL 87–346 has not been achieved. There is still temporary legislation validating existing dual-rate contracts, and the fact that shipowners have been prevented from establishing new and effective contract systems to meet changing patterns of trade has meant that the effectiveness of the conference tie has been steadily reduced.

In addition to all this, section 15 under which agreements might be approved by the FMC was rewritten so as to make it more restrictive, virtually prohibiting inter-conference agreements (e.g. between the east and west coasts of the USA) such as the Celler Committee called 'super-conferences', and explicitly providing that no conference agreement should be approved unless it allowed entry on equal terms of other 'qualified' carriers in the trade. The qualifications to be required were not defined and in practice virtually none are required.

A further amendment to section 15 of the 1916 Act required the FMC to disapprove any agreement, whether previously approved by it or not, 'on a finding of inadequate policing of the obligations under it...' The curiously uncertain wording was agreed only after a considerable amount of argument. By its vagueness it was almost certain to cause trouble; this is dealt with below.

The purpose of this amendment was to overcome the lack of effective jurisdiction by the FMC in Washington. 'Self-policing' a conference agreement involves the carriers concerned agreeing upon rules by which an independent firm, usually accountants, has the right of access and investigation into the affairs of any member of the agreement who is alleged to have broken the agreement, e.g. by cutting freight rates in one way or another. The neutral body, of course, must have the power to make its judgments effective, usually by levying fines.

Section 16 of the Act was amended to allow State Governors to protest to the FMC that freight rates or tariff rules discriminated unjustly against their territories; whereupon the FMC was to order the conference concerned to show cause why the rate or rule should not be set aside.

A completely new section, 18 (*b*), was introduced compelling carriers to file their tariffs with the FMC in Washington, to make them available to the public, not to raise their rates without giving 30 days notice to the FMC (which could, however, waive this 30 days requirement) and not to lower their rates without first filing a tariff amendment with the FMC. This section also required the FMC to control the form and manner in which tariffs should be filed and to reject any tariff not conforming with these rules. Upon rejection the use of a tariff was to become unlawful. The FMC was also required to disapprove any rate which it found to be unreasonably high or low or detrimental to the commerce of the USA.

Section 20 of the Shipping Act, which prohibits carriers and their agents from receiving or disclosing information about shipments or their routing, was amended to allow this information to be disclosed to the conference, or any agency employed by the conference, to decide whether a dual-rate contract or the conference agreement itself had been breached.

A new section 43 was introduced giving the FMC power to make rules necessary for carrying out the provisions of the Act.

The administration of PL 87–346

Many of these provisions are still highly controversial, and from many different points of view. Equally important, however, has been the tightening of the FMCs whole attitude to its task of administering the Act and regulating the shipping industry. Before PL 87–346 was enacted the regulation of the steamship industry and those associated with it, like terminals and forwarding agents, was carried out by a staff of twenty-five to thirty people. The port terminal industry was 'regulated' by one man and a trainee. By November 1961 the staff of the FMC Office of Regulation had increased to fifty, and it was planned to double this.[1] The FMC budget is now in the region of £1 million per year; shipowners who sometimes maintain that the FMC writes bad law and issues rules that are *ultra vires*, both in the national context of the USA and in the wider sphere of international law, and who contest its decisions in the US courts, complain that this budget is difficult to compete with.

The radical change in this administration and in the attitude of foreign governments and shipowners to the 1916 Shipping Act since the passage of PL 87–346 is exemplified in the following exchange, which took place during the oral examination of the British shipowners' delegation by the Bonner Committee, which was then considering an early draft of PL 87–346: 'Mr Keville (leader of the delegation): "I think I can say that *as it has been administered* in the past we have not found the 1916 Act unacceptable." The Chairman (Rep. Bonner, Dem.): "That is where we find ourselves in a difficulty. *The 1916 Act has not been administered.*"' Certainly, attempts have been made to administer it since 1961.

Although one of the commissioners is a retired admiral, the FMC staff consists largely of lawyers. From the content and form of its arguments it is clear that it employs no economists; or, if it does, that they have no power. From the economist's point of view, therefore, many of its arguments are curious. Thus, for example, it is quite legal to fix freight rates so as to discriminate according to value between commodities which, from the point of view of the carrier, are technically identical, but it is illegal to discriminate between shippers or consignees. In so far, however, as many commodities have only one, or only a few, shippers, this can amount to exactly the same thing. Certainly, the monopsonistic power of

[1] Speech by L. F. Fuller, Chief of the Division of Foreign Regulation, to North Atlantic Ports Association meeting, 15 November 1961.

large firms, like the motor manufacturers, is evident in the tariff structures of conferences in the outward trades from the USA.

Section 15 agreements

Considering the quantity of legal brainpower employed by the FMC it is surprising that it is comparatively easy to avoid at least some of the requirements of the Shipping Act. Section 15, for example, is objected to by many shipowners, who do not care to have their agreements with their competitors on file in Washington, subject to hearings and legal arguments, and open to the public view. This section is said to require the filing of agreements between companies of which one is a parent and the other a wholly owned subsidiary, or which are both subsidiaries of the same parent, since, in either case, two different legal personalities are involved. (There appears to be little or no case law on this point, but this is the burden of both counsel's advice and the FMCs own precedents in approving such agreements.) The fleets may well be operated as one (and perhaps thay may even have the same directors and staff) and there is necessarily a constant flow of consultations and agreements, changing according to the requirements of the trades concerned.

Yet, under section 15, agreements may have to be filed, with lawyers' advice to be taken and considered, and FMC approval to be obtained. Not unnaturally, perhaps, those concerned with this type of situation rapidly cease to appreciate its Gilbertian qualities. FMC approval, even where the agreement is not contentious and no amendments are required, may take five or six months to obtain. It is not hard to imagine that such a brake on a group's operations would not be tolerated. If this is true then unfiled agreements would be the result. This, of course, would be illegal, though it was quite common before PL 87–346 was enacted. Any such illegalities render the operators subject to fines, in respect of each such agreement, of up to $1000 per day, a further dampening of the humour inherent in the situation.

Of the various devices for avoiding the requirements of section 15, one of the simplest may be mentioned here. The FMC has held[1] that

[1] The Grace-Viking case, FMO Dockets 946, 950, 953 reported in CIB—15 November 1962.

shareholders in a company are not operating an unfiled (and therefore illegal) section 15 agreement. Any two or more companies wishing to co-operate in any way, therefore, can form a jointly owned company to which they then charter their ships. The FMC will recognize only one legal person and no co-operation.

Nevertheless, although the provisions of section 15 can sometimes be avoided, doing so complicates the affairs of the companies involved very greatly, and generally slows down the process of adjustment to changing circumstances.

It is noteworthy that the practices prohibited by section 15, and other sections of the Act, are allowed to American shipowners in trades which do not touch the USA. Naturally, they take full advantage of this; one of them, American President Lines, belongs to 59 conferences, of which 25 are in trades not touching the USA; of the latter, 11 use deferred loyalty rebates.

Viewed as anti-monopoly legislation one of the most remarkable provisions of section 15 is that, while it requires the filing of all agreements between common carriers operating in the foreign commerce of the USA, and requires the FMC to disapprove agreements that it finds to be 'unjustly discriminatory or unfair as between carriers, shippers, exporters, importers or ports, or between exporters from the USA and their foreign competitors or to operate to the detriment of the commerce of the USA, or contrary to the public interest', it requires the FMC to approve *all* other agreements. There is thus no 'presumption of guilt', such as is found in the Anti-Trust Acts, or in the British Restrictive Practices Act of 1956; instead there is a presumption of innocence and not necessarily any trial. Moreover, neither the Act nor the FMC make any distinction between horizontal and vertical agreements. Obviously, many of the vertical agreements it considers are simply contracts made in the ordinary conduct of business.

Even the legal meaning of many of these phrases is most unclear. Ignoring the justification for conferences mentioned above, it could be, but is not, argued by the FMC that the commerce of the USA would benefit from freight rates that were low and fluctuating on the grounds that the lower your delivered price the more goods you sell, and that flexibility of rates is the best way of ensuring rapid response to changing requirements. On the contrary, the FMC argues that the foreign commerce of the USA benefits from freight rates that are stable, and, at least by implication, higher than if the agreements it approved did not exist. American shippers, large and small, appeared before the Bonner Committee to argue for stable freight rates too, and most of them appeared as strong supporters of the conference system, though the Justice Department has publicly suspected that this is merely one way of reducing competition between shippers. Thus, although there are several good economic reasons in favour of establishing the legality of inter-carrier agreements in seaborne trade, they do not appear to be known to the FMC. In so far as the right thing is done perhaps it is better that it should be done on fallacious grounds than that it should not be done at all.

Unfortunately, even if the right thing is done, it involves considerable delay. As noted above, FMC approval of the simplest agreement may often take six months to obtain, and the preparation of the agreement may take six months beforehand, often involving consultation with FMC staff on what is likely to be acceptable, and advice from a firm of American lawyers specializing in this subject. (A British shipowner recently remarked that one of his objections to the law was that he couldn't do anything without asking his lawyer first and it cost him a thousand dollars each time he did so.) Clearly, these delays are a considerable impediment to the ordinary progress of business. They bring the FMC into disrepute and it is not clear that they serve any useful purpose whatever.

Furthermore, the provisos in PL 87–346 on the characteristics of agreements which must not be approved are remarkably one-sided. 'Not operate to the detriment of the commerce of the United States'? Does this include the US shipowners? Or is it confined to importers and exporters? Even if we knew what it meant, even if Congress (or the FMC) gave any signs of knowing what they meant by it, what about the commerce of other countries? What about the public interest of other countries?

Self-policing—a study in futile regulation

A clear example of the time-wasting that arises out of these vague phrases concerns the provision of section 15 that the FMC shall disapprove any agreement on a finding of inadequate policing of the obligations under it. Does this mean that the FMC can disapprove an agreement on this ground when it is submitted? Or do they have to wait for evidence of inadequate policing after it has been operating for some time? Moreover, no one has ever discovered what 'inadequate policing' means. Some shipowners have maintained that adequacy is a relative term and in this context can only be relative to the necessity. From this it follows that if there is no question of the obligations under an agreement having been broken (e.g. by the giving of secret rebates to shippers), there is no need for any policing arrangements at all.

The FMC, acting under its rule-making powers of section 43, issued comprehensive draft rules[1] for the establishment of self-policing agencies in March 1962. Curiously, these rules were silent on the major point at issue, that of whether section 15 required formal self-policing arrangements to be established, or whether the argument of adequacy being relative to the necessity was valid. The rules specified that the prior approval of the FMC must be sought, and went on to describe the conditions under which the self-policing agency was to work. One of these required the agency to report to the FMC on its findings in all complaints referred to it, together with full details; and any documents concerned, whether in the possession of the self-policing agency or of the lines concerned, were to be available to the FMC as and when required.

Once again comments and protests poured in from all over the world. In the first place the rules said nothing about the geographical situation of the self-policing agency, nor did they place any limitation on the ability of the FMC to demand documents made available to that agency by the conference lines. Clearly, a government agency can only obtain documents physically located within the jurisdiction of another state by agreement of their owners or by permission of that state. But it is equally clear that if an agency of one government is to attempt to regulate an essentially international industry then it cannot do so effectively with access only to one end of it. If the FMC can legally demand documents located abroad then it is infringing the jurisdiction of other countries: if it cannot get them then Congress has set the FMC an impossible task.

[1] Docket 986, Federal Register, 24 March 1962.

This problem has arisen in other contexts. In July 1960 the FMB, under the severe prodding of the Celler Committee, issued an order under section 21 of the 1916 Act requiring about 400 named carriers, mostly foreign, to produce all agreements involving the waterborne commerce of the USA including those made with firms and individuals outside the USA, and apparently even with foreign governments. This was objected to by most of the respondents, and their governments, who appealed in two groups.

Appeals from decisions of the FMC can be made to the Federal Courts of Appeal. The two appeals, in different courts, produced opposite decisions. In the one the FMC order was held void for vagueness, since it failed to specify the purpose for which the documents were required, and in the other it was upheld. Neither court paid much attention to the jurisdiction question, saying that was a matter for the executive branch. The FMC subsequently cancelled the order as having been made unfair, being applicable to some respondents and not to others. If the case had been decided by the Supreme Court the judgment might have followed the dictum of Mr Chief Justice Marshall in 'The Charming Betsy' case,[1] that '...an act of Congress ought never to be construed to violate the law of nations if any other possible construction remains', quoted and relied upon by the Supreme Court as recently as 17 February 1963[2] which added '...therefore...for us to sanction the exercise of local sovereignty (by the USA)...in this delicate field of international relations there must be present the affirmative intention of Congress clearly expressed'. Congress is clearly silent on this question as far as the text of the Shipping Act, 1916, is concerned.

The UK Minister of Transport forbade the British respondents to that section 21 order to produce any of the documents located outside the USA. Other governments, in this and other cases involving the same principle, have acted similarly although the Italian Government has gone so far as to make a permanent prohibition, covering all future FMC orders as well as any current ones. In other cases some

---

[1] 6, US (2 Cranch), 64, 118 (1804).
[2] In a case involving the jurisdiction of the National Labour Relations Board over foreign seafarers on vessels registered in other countries—Dockets 91, 93 and 107.

compromise has generally been found by which the respondents said they would promise not to do whatever they were accused of any more if the FMC would drop its request for documents.

Clearly, if the foreign lines do not have to produce documents located outside the USA then they have a certain immunity from the 1916 Act. This would involve the US lines being more strictly regulated than their foreign competitors, a position which was certainly not the object of either Rep. Celler or Rep. Bonner. Yet if the FMC does have the power to compel production of documents located abroad then the USA would be compulsorily exporting its own theories of government to other countries.

The second main objection to the draft self-policing rules was that they involved double jeopardy. Under the Fifth Amendment to the USA Constitution 'no person shall...be subject for the same offence to be twice put in jeopardy of life or limb...' ('limb' clearly includes property). Under the proposed rules a self-policing agency would have the power to fine an offender; if the agency then had to furnish full details, including documents located abroad, to the FMC, proceedings might well be started against the offender by either the FMC or the Department of Justice and a second punishment inflicted. Moreover, the FMC would have obtained documents located abroad through, as it were, the back door.

The outcome of all these arguments, which involved considerable legal expenses both by the FMC and by the governments, conferences and individual shipowners concerned, was that on 29 January 1963, more than ten months after the draft regulations were promulgated, the FMC withdrew them entirely, as an expression of 'confidence in the desire and ability of the conferences to eliminate malpractices in their respective trades', and on the grounds that 'detailed regulation may be unnecessary at this time'.[1]

On 12 March 1963, however, the FMC returned to the subject with completely new proposed regulations,[2] much shorter than the earlier ones and, at first sight, open to none of the earlier objections. These new proposed regulations began by paraphrasing the law,

[1] Quotations are from a statement by the FMC chairman and an FMC order, both dated 29 January 1963.
[2] Docket 1094, Federal Register of that date.

stating their intention of aiding the FMC 'in its determination as to the adequacy of the self-policing system' went on to specify that section 15 agreements *must* contain a provision describing the policing methods and concluded by requiring the production, twice a year, of reports to the FMC describing the complaints received and the action taken, but without naming the firms involved.

But in spite of their innocent appearance even these rules are open to both the earlier objections. They still appear to claim the widest possible jurisdiction, they state that policing arrangements must be established (which does not appear to be the most probable meaning of the Act), and the risk of double jeopardy still exists.

The last point arises because any reference of an alleged violation of the agreement to the 'neutral body' would normally be made at a conference meeting and must necessarily name the parties involved. The FMC insists upon receiving copies of all conference minutes and would therefore be able to take any action it pleased, irrespective of what the neutral body was doing.

Shipowners have again protested that these rules are unreasonable and *ultra vires*. Again, therefore, a year and a half after PL 87–346 became law, nothing effective has been done and the FMC is still unable to produce rules which it feels adequately and defensibly to express the law.

Conclusion

It is clear from the record of reports and hearings that the 87th Congress of the USA, in passing its Public Law 346, had three principal purposes in mind. In the first place, it intended to provide for an effective tie between carriers and shippers by means of dual-rate contract systems. Secondly, and largely as a result of the Celler hearings, it intended to make the control of monopolistic competition in the foreign-going common carrier services to and from the USA more effective. Agreeing that it was necessary to provide exemption from the Anti-Trust Acts, which are both undesirable and impracticable as far as this industry is concerned, it sought to limit the types of agreement that should be approved under Section 15 and to control their operation. Thirdly, it had what may be termed the hidden purpose, which was revealed partly in the confusion between its regulatory and its promotional functions that existed in the former FMB, and was shown with startling clarity in the remark of Rep. Bonner quoted on page 28. This purpose was to enhance, or at least to maintain, the US merchant fleet without increasing the subsidy cost to the taxpayers.

It is equally clear that the Act has succeeded in none of these purposes. It is, indeed, doubtful whether they can be achieved by legislative action.

If the first of these purposes could have been carried out under the terms of PL 87–346 (and in view of the restrictive provisions quoted above this is doubtful) it has been frustrated by the actions of the FMC in attempting to impose regulations upon the industry; these regulations have been the subject of numerous protests, though it is difficult to say whether the volume and nature of the protests is changing because the FMC appears to have stopped publishing them. Presumably the FMC, as a result of these protests, are unable to make up their minds as to what the law does require or permit them to do, for in a year and a half they have neither produced regulations which satisfied the industry nor which they were prepared to defend in the courts. This apparent inability of the FMC to decide what the law means underlines the difficulty experienced by all the foreign shipowners affected by it, that they do not know when they are acting legally or illegally; that the views of legal experts are often at variance with one another; and that it would take many years for the courts to define what the phraseology of the Act means.

It is very doubtful if this purpose could be achieved at all adequately by anything except a brief Act stating that dual-rate contract systems in the foreign-going seaborne commerce of the USA should be legal. After this had been in operation for a few years the possibility of any abuses of the system could then be looked at.

The second of these purposes has also been frustrated. It has already been demonstrated that the provisions of section 15 are quite easy to avoid even without breaking the law, by any willing to complicate their business sufficiently. Moreover, the simple process of not filing one's agreements is a perfectly adequate answer to any problems raised by this legislation, at least as far as the non-American shipowner is concerned. This may be illegal under US law, but, if the parties to the agreement are not US citizens, and the documents concerned are located outside the USA, America has no jurisdiction. Moreover, even if the US courts should, at some future date, hold that they do have this jurisdiction then by no stretch of the legal imagination can the FMC be regarded as having the power to inspect offices and files located outside the USA in order to verify that all the documents alleged to be required have actually been produced. And without this power they are entirely dependent on the good-will of the accused in producing the evidence. Thus, whether they have the jurisdiction or not they cannot possibly make it effective.

But the FMC certainly does have the power to compel US citizens to produce documents. The effect of the monopoly control provisions of the Shipping Act of 1916, as amended, is therefore more rigorous against US liner operators than against foreign shipowners.

This clearly conflicts with the third purpose of PL 87–346, that of assisting the American shipowners. It is difficult to judge whether this has been achieved but in view of the fact that all the American shipowners involved are liner operators, that they are encouraged by the Maritime Administration to join conferences, that the point of legalizing dual-rate systems was to assist conferences (which has, quite clearly, not succeeded) it is very likely that they have been harmed by this legislation rather than the reverse.

This appears to be true in spite of the widespread suspicion that the FMC is biased in their favour. If this is true then the bias would seem to be a hangover from the confusion which existed in the former FMB before the eminently sensible separation of its two functions. Foreign shipowners, in conducting what amount to negotiations with the FMC, find it of great advantage to have an American operator on their side, since the subsidized line can always approach the Maritime Administration on any aspect of their operations and they, in turn, are, as it were, next door to the FMC and possess all the contacts which usually exist between government departments.

Evidence for this suspicion exists in three speeches made since both the Presidential Reorganization Plan No. 7 and PL 87–346 came into effect. The first was made by Admiral Harllee, vice-chairman of the FMC, to a body called 'The Maritime Association of Greater

Boston'[1] on 22 May 1962, when he openly promoted US flag shipping, advocating that US businessmen should ship more cargo by
American ships to help the balance of payments, because of the sales
promotions services operated on behalf of shippers by American
steamship lines and because US ships offered service as good as, or
better than, foreign ships at the same (conference) rates. He said
nothing of the American seafarers' greater proclivity to go on strike
and thereby to delay shipments routed by US ships. The second of
these speeches was made by the FMC chairman, Mr Stakem, to the
FMC staff, when he said[2] *inter alia:* 'We seek equitable regulations to
assure the existence of an American Merchant Marine to serve our
business community and to bolster our nation's vital ocean defenses',
adding with unusual modesty that 'we still face the challenge of full
understanding and compliance with our shipping laws'. One presumes
that the FMC staff bore his remarks in mind for the future. The third
of these speeches[3] was made by Mr J. V. Day, a member of the FMC
in New York on 18 April 1963. He said, *inter alia:* 'We must sell the
proposition that a strong merchant marine is a must in this country
in time of peace as well as in time of emergency...'

These are all remarkable statements, coming as they do from people
in quasi-judicial positions; and these three gentlemen constitute a
majority in the FMC.

Yet, in spite of the complexity of the legal arguments and procedures, the rub of the matter remains, from the practical point of
view, in the jurisdiction question. It is universally agreed that a
nation has the right to regulate her own foreign commerce if she
wants to; to impose tariffs, quotas and prohibitions, whether discriminatory or not, and to impose any restrictions on her own citizens
and citizens of other countries within her own territories. But she does
not have the right to regulate the actions of foreign citizens outside
her own territories whether they are taking part in her own foreign
commerce or not. Britain may regulate the activities of Smithfield
Market as much as she pleases, but if, say, Australian and Argentinian
meat producers were to have a price agreement there is nothing
legally speaking, that she could do about it.

[1] Reported in CIB, 22 May 1962.   [2] Reported in CIB, 10 August 1962.
[3] Reported in CIB, 18 April 1963.

Not only does no nation have that right, but if one claims it she cannot exercise it without interfering with the jurisdiction of at least one other nation. Whatever its rights and wrongs, a policy of *laissez-faire* is just as much a policy, and just as valid a policy, as any other. If, when two nations trade together, one unilaterally arrogates to itself the right to regulate that trade then she is necessarily conflicting with the policy of the second nation. In order to produce a conflict of jurisdiction it is, therefore, quite unnecessary to imagine circumstances in which the countries at each end of a trade regulate it in contradictory ways.

Clearly, however, if both countries do regulate the trade between them, and without first co-ordinating their policies closely, then utter confusion, leading to a total breakdown of commerce, may well be the result. Unfortunately, it seems possible that certain other nations may enact legislation which would have this effect. The British Restrictive Practices Act of 1956 refers specifically to the supply of goods and thereby excludes services like shipping, but Australia is currently considering proposals for a similar act which may include shipping. Considering that the USA is the largest importer of Australian meat, to say nothing of her importance as an importer of wool, lead, rutile sand and other commodities, the disruption of the trade between the two countries seems the last thing to be desired.

It is difficult not to conclude that PL 87–346 and the original Shipping Act of 1916 were written by lawyers and for lawyers, and that as they sit in their legal oases they little seem to realize that they have many carriers so scared of the law's intricacies that they are inhibited from providing services, or extensions to services, which would be fully justified by ordinary commercial standards. Thus the law damages the commerce between the USA and other countries and the public interest suffers accordingly.

3

INVESTMENT IN SHIPPING AND THE BALANCE OF PAYMENTS: A CASE-STUDY OF IMPORT-SUBSTITUTION POLICY[1]

Nations with more or less chronic shortages of foreign currencies sometimes consider investment in merchant shipping as a way of improving matters. In discussions on the subject three assertions are often made or implied:

(1) That investment in shipping will improve the balance of payments;

(2) That shipping possesses some characteristic which makes this effect particularly large, even when the return on capital is smaller than that obtainable elsewhere;

(3) That the benefit to the balance of payments is greater when the ships operate in cross-trades[2] (i.e. on voyages which do not involve calls in the ships' home country).

The object of this paper is to examine the extent to which these effects exist and to provide a simple method by which they may be estimated for any particular set of circumstances. This method is based upon the most likely combination of circumstances but may be varied to suit any others. Worked examples are included as an appendix.

The method suggested here is applicable not only to decisions to create new fleets but also to decisions concerning the expansion or contraction of existing fleets and to decisions to withdraw from merchant shipping. Although it proceeds by a detailed analysis to some very simple conclusions, the detail is thought necessary because

---

[1] I am indebted to Mr F. E. Harmer, Mr T. L. Higgins, Dr R. Hope and Professor S. G. Sturmey for commenting on earlier drafts of this paper.

[2] See e.g. *Japan shipping and shipbuilding*, April 1963: 'When a Japanese ship is engaged in the transportation of cargo between ports of loading and discharge other than those of Japan, namely cross-trade, the freightage earned thereby represents a *net* foreign exchange revenue; it adds to Japan's credit, which is short of requirements'. (Author's italics.)

when the above assertions are made or implied they are rarely accompanied by any analysis at all.

There are several ways of defining the effect of investing in ships on the balance of payments;[1] most are either wrong or misleading. To ask: How much foreign exchange will the fleet earn? is to omit all mention of the foreign exchange costs of running the fleet. Yet to ask: What will be the net excess of foreign exchange earnings over foreign exchange expenses? is still wrong, for some of the ships' earnings may not be received in foreign exchange and, if the national-flag ships replace foreign ones, there will be a loss of foreign exchange formerly earned by providing the latter with port services.

Obviously, the proper question is: What is the net extent to which the balance of payments differs from what it would have been if the investment in ships had not taken place? This net difference is the resultant of a large number of separate effects; these may, however, be classified under four headings, of which the first is a credit to the balance of payments and the other three are either debits or zero according to the circumstances of the case.

(*a*) *Freight.* If we consider a nation which has a significant part of its foreign trade carried in foreign ships, then, in so far as the freight in either direction is being paid by its own residents, the substitution of national for foreign ships must mean a saving of foreign exchange. In so far as the freight earned by the foreign ships is being paid by residents of foreign countries, the earnings of the national ships must mean new foreign exchange earnings. If the substitution takes place in a cross-trade then presumably this second point will apply to the whole of the freight. Precisely the same arguments apply to passenger fares, mail-money and any other gross earnings. Thus the whole of the revenue, in both directions, and whether in a

---

[1] The point has been examined, in the context of British shipping, by Professor S. G. Sturmey, *British shipping and world competition*, London, 1963, and in a wider context by John Seland, *EFTA Bulletin*, June 1962. Both have called attention to the misleading qualities of most published statistics from the point of view of shipping policy decisions. For earlier studies, see J. S. Smith, *Foreign Commerce Weekly* (Washington, DC), 22 September 1945; H. F. Karreman, *Methods of improving world transportation accounts applied to 1950–53*, Technical Paper 15, National Bureau of Economic Research, USA, 1961, and *Rev. Econ. and Statist.*, February 1958 (Supplement); and articles by I. S. Lloyd in *The Times*, 5 and 6 July 1961.

cross-trade or not, becomes a gain to the balance of payments. Any distinction between shipments made f.o.b. and c.i.f. is irrelevant.

It may be noted, however, that what is relevant is the freight currently being earned by the foreign ships. If investment in shipping is accompanied by protection, e.g. flag discrimination, which results in higher freight rates in the protected market, it is no longer the earnings of the national-flag ships which represent a gain to the balance of payments: it is the earnings of the foreign ships which could replace them without protection and at lower freight rates.[1] This point is equally important in considering the reservation of coastal trades (cabotage).[2]

In a world of unconvertible, or only partly convertible, currencies, however, it is possible that either the saving or the gains in foreign exchange (or both) may appear in some particularly desirable currency. This possibility depends not on nominal but on *de facto* non-convertibility and the absence of currency 'leaks'. Moreover, if a given currency is especially desirable to one nation, it is probably so to several others and there may, therefore, be correspondingly intense competition to enter shipping services in which freight can be received in that currency, thus reducing the profits, which, as is shown below, are an important component of the net result.

---

[1] The discussion here assumes that if higher freight rates are charged on exports they cannot be passed on to the consumer, either because the c.i.f. price is effectively determined by competition from other sources of supply or because full advantage has already been taken of any monopolistic position. There is no reason why a monopolistic situation should be created or altered simply because the goods move under a different flag. Similar assumptions are made about imports. Thus the gains caused by flag discrimination in the shipping account of the balance of payments will be precisely offset by losses in the visible trade account. The only exception to this situation appears when export trade is being hampered by physically inadequate shipping services. Then it is possible that the overall trade-plus-shipping accounts may improve the balance of payments and provide some profits even though the shipping component alone may do neither. But there are usually some shipowners looking for such circumstances and willing to provide services at a loss in the early years if they are convinced that the trade will ultimately be profitable. Given the doctrine of the freedom of the seas it does not matter, as far as the trade component is concerned, where these shipowners come from.

[2] An example of an occasion when this point may have been acted upon by the USA shipping authorities was cited by the author in an earlier paper: 'USA legislation and the foreign shipowner: A critique', reprinted above. pp. 25–45.

(*b*) *Spending abroad.* Unless they are engaged in purely coastal trade the national-flag ships will inevitably have expenses outside their own country. Unless the nation is an oil producer they will have to purchase bunkers abroad (indeed, even if it is an oil producer they will normally have to purchase some fuel abroad) and in any case they will incur port dues, agents' commissions, cargo-handling costs and various other items of which the largest will usually be insurance, some repairs and the personal spending of the crew. A large part of these items is therefore foreign exchange expenditure incurred as a result of the substitution and must be deducted from the first item. If the ships enter a cross-trade they will incur almost all of their running expenses (except crews' wages remitted home) in foreign exchange. Thus, where cross-trades are concerned, this item will be much larger than it would be if a direct out-and-home trade were concerned.

(*c*) *Spending at home.* Except where they are fully occupied in cross-trades the new ships will spend large sums in their home territory. These will not enter directly into the balance of payments, but in so far as they replace the spending of foreign ships which formerly carried the trade, they represent a loss of foreign exchange which would otherwise have been earned. For much the same reasons as those given above, the foreign ships cannot have avoided spending large sums in the nations whose ports they visited.

In other words, all items of expenditure on current goods and services which do not change the location of the expenditure upon the substitution of a national-flag ship for a foreign one must appear either under (*b*) above or (*c*) above. It does not, however, greatly matter which, since both must be deducted from the foreign exchange earned or saved under the first of these headings.[1]

There appear to be four circumstances in which expenditure on current goods and services may change its location following the

[1] Apart from these effects, and in so far as any expenditure in the home country comes out of newly generated income, there will be a general increase in imports, dependent upon the marginal propensity to import of the income-recipients. In so far as they buy exportable goods, moreover, any export surplus may be reduced. But neither of these arguments will apply to that part of incomes which is not newly generated unless it involves shifts of income from those with a low marginal propensity to import to those with a high marginal propensity to import.

4

substitution. The first is that some large part of the crews' wages is normally spent in the countries in which the members of the crew are resident. They will spend it in advances of wages before joining the ship, in allotments of pay or cash sent home to support their families or for other purposes and they will often have part of their wages deducted as tax and as social-security contributions. If, therefore, the crews of the new ships are normally resident in the nation investing in those ships, and if this was not true of the foreign ships which formerly carried the trade, the place where the crews' wages are spent will change. Normally, however, this part will be significantly less than the whole cost of crew wages because the foreign crew would have spent some money in the country with which we are concerned and because the crew of the national-flag ship will spend some money outside their own country. If, for example, the proportions are 10 % in each case, and if the levels of the crew costs (taking account both of differences in earnings and of manning scales) are the same, then 10 % of crew costs will appear under (*b*) above and 10 % under (*c*) above. But if the new ship enters a cross-trade, then the crew must be expected to spend more outside their own country. Thus, for ships in cross-trades, the total deduction might be 20 % of crew costs under (*b*) above and none under (*c*) above; i.e. it would still total the same as it would in a direct trade.

The second possibility of an item of expenditure on current goods and services appearing under neither of these headings concerns management costs. If the management of the new ship (apart from agencies, which are usually remunerated by commissions) is located in the investing nation, then the associated costs will be transferred from a foreign country to the home territory. In practice this is very likely, though, as with crew costs, it depends on there being a sufficient number of trained men available.

The third possibility is that with the change in the place of management there will be some change in the location of purchases, e.g. of ships' stores. This will arise partly out of convenience and partly out of changes in effective prices; inspection of goods is more expensive at a distance. Valid though this point may be, it can apply only to a few items of running expenses, e.g. stores and food. These, as is shown in the appendix, are relatively small proportions of total costs; and it is unlikely that the proportionate effect on them would be very large. This possibility may therefore be ignored without significant error.

The fourth possibility is that, by introducing discriminatory controls, it will be possible to reduce foreign exchange spending by the national-flag ships. At first sight this is an attractive possibility, for Table 3.1 (*a*) in the appendix shows that, in the example cited, losses to the balance of payments under 'new spending' are well over half the total losses. A closer look reveals that the imposition of discriminatory controls is impossible on many items and difficult on the rest. Commissions represent selling costs and must be incurred where the customer is located; cargo handling and fuel costs, canal tolls and port charges are similarly impossible to affect, and in the example quoted in the appendix (Table 3.1 (*a*) and (*b*)) these leave only 16 % of balance of payments debits amenable to control. Controls on crew spending are strongly resented and reduce the attractiveness of a sea-going career; moreover, they are easily evaded by any of a number of methods, of which a bank or a *bureau de change* is the simplest and the illegal selling of ships' stores the most expensive. Provisions can certainly be bought at home; this is the only item which normally presents no difficulty for control, but in the example quoted it represents less than 2 % of total debits to the balance of payments. Ships' stores are often of a specialized nature and manufactured only in certain countries; or they may be wanted urgently. They, too, represent less than 2 % of foreign exchange debits in the example given in the appendix. With repairs the situation is hardly easier, for many of these are urgent or require specialized services. Insurance requires a specialized market; this is why most ships are either insured or reinsured in London (sometimes New York) and these are also the headquarters of the principal Protection and Indemnity Clubs (which are mutual insurance associations covering certain risks not insurable on the open market—cargo and crew claims, etc.). Even if all these items were subject to really rigorous controls, it is doubtful whether the difference made to the data presented in the appendix would be greater than one percentage point of the ratios shown there.

(*d*) *Capital.* The fourth element which may well affect the balance of payments concerns the capital cost of the ships. If the investing nation simply purchases them abroad, then the immediate result of a decision to substitute national for foreign ships is a large outflow of foreign exchange. Obviously, this is the last thing to be desired. If the ships can be built wholly within the home territory or obtained from abroad as gifts, then this fourth effect on the balance of payments will be zero. Between these two extremes there is a wide range of possibilities. Towards one end the ships can be purchased abroad on credit terms of varying types. At the other end of the range of possibilities the ship may indeed be built at home but this will be physically possible only if there is a shipbuilding industry capable of building ships of the appropriate type and size. Even where this is so, however, it is quite probable that some components (e.g. winches, windlasses, radio and radar equipment, generators, steering gear and, conceivably, even the main engine) may have to be imported from abroad. Even if they are not imported from abroad, it may be necessary to import specialized technicians, with salaries and expatriation expenses payable in foreign exchange, or to pay licence fees for the manufacture of equipment to foreign designs. Such arrangements are quite common even in highly developed shipbuilding countries.[1]

While the first three of these effects on the balance of payments are likely to be roughly constant (in real terms) over the life of the ship, except for reductions in earnings and, possibly, higher foreign exchange payments for repairs in the fifth, ninth, thirteenth, seventeenth and twenty-first years of ship life, when the quadrennial surveys (which are of increasing severity) fall due, that associated with capital is highly variable and is largely within the control of the investing country. Control can be exercised by obtaining the ships as part of an aid programme, or on credit terms of varying types and at such rates of interest as may be obtainable by negotiation. As yet another alternative the ships can be obtained secondhand, when their operating lives under the new flat will be shorter, the repair costs somewhat higher and the initial cost correspondingly

---

[1] '...most (conventional) ships built today contain engines made by firms who have not designed them...the design frequently is foreign'. *Nuclear power for ship propulsion: report of the working group on marine nuclear research*, Cmnd. 2358, HMSO 1964, para. 46 (iii).

less. It does not, therefore, follow that second-hand ships will necessarily make larger net contributions to the balance of payments.

The logical way to decide upon the best method of improving the balance of payments in a long term is, therefore:

(*a*) To consider all the alternative courses of action. These must include non-shipping activities as well as the various forms of activity in shipping and the various ways of financing them.

(*b*) To express all these in terms of net present value[1] by discounting, at an appropriate rate, the net effects in each year of the projects' lives to a common base year. Any negative effects due to initial costs must, of course, be included in the calculations.

The project with the greatest net present value is the best. The process is precisely the same as any other present value calculation except that it is the net favourable effect on the balance of payments that is being maximized, not the net present value of cash flows.

The comparison with non-shipping activities is particularly important at the present time. In the examples shown in the appendix the net contributions to the balance of payments consist of 80 % of wages, plus the contribution to those overhead costs (including management) which are not payable abroad. In Table 3.1 (*a*) and (*b*) this contribution includes an element of profit which, if defined so as to exclude interest, is not payable abroad (unless the investing country financed the fleet abroad on equity terms). The net contribu-

---

[1] Early discussions of the theory and practice of discounting cash flows to net present values are cited by R. Turvey in 'Present Value versus Internal Rate of Return' *Economic Journal*, May 1963. An excellent and up-to-date work on the subject is Merrett and Sykes' *The finance and analysis of capital projects* (Longmans, 1963), though, like most of the literature on the topic, it deals with net present value only in its normal context of maximizing the net present value of cash flows. Where the capital cost is represented in only one payment, net present value is defined by

$$\text{NPV} = \sum_{i=1}^{i=n} \frac{A_i}{(1+r)^i} - C,$$

where *i* is the year of the project's life,
  A is the end-year cash flow,
  r is the rate of discount applicable and
  C is the capital cost

(quoted from Merrett and Sykes, *op. cit.*, p. 35). By using the analysis suggested in this paper the formula can be adapted so as to make the balance of payments effect into the maximand.

tion to the balance of payments, therefore, while it has other and possibly larger components, varies with the level of profits obtainable.

At the present time, and indeed since 1957, shipping has been experiencing low freight rates on the open market, correspondingly intense competition in the liner trades and low profits throughout the industry. This is true not only of Britain but also of other major maritime nations, whose cost levels (in ships of similar types) are much the same.

In the examples given in the appendix the ratio of improvement in the balance of payments to gross earnings of the fleet varies from 5·4 to 35·2 %. The lower figure will be applicable if the ship is purchased from abroad on repayment terms at 6 % interest over the life of the ship, and if she is operated at the negligible net profit level currently obtainable in liner trades. The higher figure will be applicable if the ship is either received as a gift or built within the investing country without imported components, technicians or know-how, and operated on a level of profits thought sufficient to attract capital into the industry and to maintain it there. In exceptionally profitable periods the improvement in the balance of payments could be greater than the higher of these figures.

The assertions quoted in the introduction can now be appraised:

(1) In an absolute sense, investment in shipping will indeed improve the balance of payments but faulty analysis of the effects may exaggerate the extent to which this occurs by between three and twenty times. In a relative sense this improvement will occur only if the same resources would not produce a greater improvement in some other activity.

(2) A correct analysis shows that there is no characteristic in shipping which makes this effect larger than in other industries; and the size of the improvement in the balance of payments is partly dependent on the return on capital.

(3) As far as the contribution to the balance of payments is concerned cross-trades are not, in principle, different from direct trades. Singling out cross-trades for special consideration is therefore wrong.

In short, and whatever the position between the extremes indicated above, it is obvious that this particular form of the do-it-yourself movement does not necessarily provide any cheap, quick or easy way of improving the balance of payments as compared with other (import-saving or export-producing) uses of the same resources. And unless such a comparison is made, and made properly, it is quite possible that investment in shipping will not improve the balance of payments: it may make the balance of payments worse than it need have been.

Appendix

This appendix contains worked examples of the method of analysing the four effects on the balance of payments which will result from the substitution of a national-flag ship for a foreign one. They are confined to the analysis of the balance of payments effects in the average year of a ship's life and do not include the process of discounting to present values advocated in the text. This is for two reasons: first, although the details of ship costs shown here go considerably beyond those previously published,[1] they are still insufficient to provide an analysis for each year of the typical ship's life; secondly, the appropriate discount rate for this rather unusual application must vary considerably between different countries.

Although the cost data presented here are believed to be reasonably representative of cargo liners operated by major unsubsidized and unprotected maritime powers, they are not derived from any single shipowner or trade route. They cannot necessarily, therefore, be regarded as applicable to any specific problem; neither can the results shown below and quoted in the text. They are intended merely as worked examples.

The ship considered is a typical deep-sea cargo liner of modern type, size and speed since this appears to be the context in which this problem is most usually considered. Other characteristics are:

Gross tonnage	10,000 (closed shelter deck)
Deadweight tonnage	12,500 (12,700 m. tonnes)
Speed	16 knots (29·65 k.p.h.)

---

[1] See e.g. A. R. Ferguson *et al.*: *The economic value of the US merchant marine*, Transportation Center, Northwestern University, Illinois, 1961; Dr D. L. McLachlan: 'The Price Policy of Liner Conferences', *Scottish Journal of Political Economy*, Vol. x, November 1963; Sturmey: *op. cit.*; R. M. Thwaites: 'The economics of ship time', *Trans. NE Coast Instn of Engrs and Shipbldrs*, Vol. 75, Part 3, January 1959.

Engines	Single-screw, super-charged diesel with exhaust boiler for some auxiliary services at sea and diesel generators for use in port, providing an overall specific fuel consumption of 0·36 lb per s.h.p. hour at sea and 2 tons per day in port both at an average of 100s. per ton of heavy fuel oil. (US $14.00)
Cargo capacity (bale)	650,000 ft³ (18,395 m³)
Crew	42

This number of crew and the level of crew costs assumed below imply some use of automatic and self-recording devices and fairly extensive use of the crew on maintenance tasks, in preference to shore labour. (The *overtime* rate for a British able-seaman is 4s. 10d. per hour;[1] this is significantly below the *straight-time* earnings for UK ship-repair and shipbuilding workers with comparable skills).[2]

The voyage is, throughout, assumed to involve transits of the Suez Canal. Although this may appear to 'load' the exercise so as to reduce the contribution to the balance of payments, in fact it does not do so. First, transit of the Suez Canal normally involves passing very close to Aden, which is one of the cheapest bunker ports in the world. Voyages through Panama, where canal tolls are slightly lower, usually involve passing near Curaçao, where bunker prices are also lower than elsewhere. Secondly, the 'cost-plus' method of arriving at earnings involves reflecting all increases in costs as increases in earnings.

The ship is assumed to spend 60 % of her time in port[3] and to operate at an average load factor of 80 % of bale capacity. She is assumed to be operated on an ordinary commercial basis, purchasing stores and carrying out repairs, other things being equal, wherever

[1] *National Maritime Board Yearbook*, 1964, p. 108.
[2] See e.g. *Ministry of Labour Gazette*, May 1964, where average hourly earnings, excluding overtime, varied from 7s. 2·9d. for shipwrights to 5s. 4·5d. for semi-skilled labourers in shipbuilding and ship-repair work.
[3] This is the figure given for ships of this type by Thwaites, *op. cit.*, and in the *Report of the committee of inquiry into the major ports of Great Britain* (Rochdale Report), Cmnd. 1824 (HMSO 1962), p. 112.

they are cheapest. It is further assumed that the foreign ships displaced from the trade were operated in the same way. While there is, therefore, room for argument as to the respective sums in the 'losses' columns of the tables their total is determined by these two assumptions. As noted in the text, they are both debits, therefore the total is what really matters. It is assumed that the crew of a ship on a direct trade spends 10 % of the wages cost in foreign countries and that the crew of a ship on a cross-trade spends 20 % because they are away from home for much longer periods.

In Table 3.1 capital charges are based on a capital cost of £1·25 mn, straight-line depreciation, a 25-year life, 6 % interest on average capital employed and profits equal to interest. This ensures that interest charges on each ship can be paid in each year of that ship's life, instead of from half-life onwards as would be the case if interest alone were allowed on average capital employed. Although this provides a ratio of net earnings, after depreciation and before interest, to average capital of about 12 % this is probably not more than is necessary, in the long run, to attract capital to the industry and to retain it there. Revenue is assumed sufficient to cover prime and capital costs on this basis. This is equivalent to an average freight rate of £7·0 ($US 19·60) per 40 occupied cubic feet if the ship makes three round voyages per year.

But, as noted in the text, this is not representative of the situation in shipping as a whole since 1957, and, certainly, it is unrepresentative of cargo-liners. The assumed levels of revenue are equivalent to capital earnings, including depreciation, interest and profit, of £12·8 per g.r.t. per year. Sample data presented by McLachlan[1] show cargo liner companies earning £11·1 in 1958, £6·4 in 1959 and 1960 and £4·6 in 1961. The trade paper *Fairplay*, which produces detailed annual analyses of British shipping companies on a somewhat wider sample than that employed by McLachlan, shows[2] £6·0 for 1963. Profits are not currently at the levels assumed in Table 3.1, nor have they been at that level in any recent year.

[1] *Op. cit.* The annual accounts of British shipping companies are not strictly appropriate for this purpose, since some include investment income and/or make use of the Shipping Companies Exemption Order, 1948. Moreover, most companies own tramps and tankers as well as cargo liners.

[2] 9 January 1963, p. 149.

TABLE 3.1. *The balance of payment effects, in the average year of the ship's life, of substituting a national for a foreign ship* (when shipping is **profitable**). *(a)* In a *direct trade*, and *(b)* in a *cross-trade*

(£000s p.a.)

Item (1)	Ship account (2)	Gains (3)	Losses by increased spending (4)		Losses by non-receipt (5)		Total (6)
(a) and *(b)*	*(a)* and *(b)*	*(a)* and *(b)*	*(a)*	*(b)*	*(a)*	*(b)*	*(a)* and *(b)*
REVENUE (freight)	cr. 546	546					
COSTS:							
Commissions at 5%	dr. 27	—	14	27	14	—	27
Stevedoring at 25%	136	—	68	136	68	—	136
Bunkers	28	—	28	28	—	—	28
Canal tolls	13	—	13	13	—	—	13
Port charges	50	—	25	50	25	—	50
(£ per day)							
Wages 150	55	—	5	11	5	—	11
Provisions 21	8	—	4	8	4	—	8
Stores 30	11	—	5	11	5	—	11
Repairs 125	46	—	23	46	23	—	46
Insurance 55	20	—	20	20	—	—	20
Sundries	4	—	2	4	2	—	4
Management	20	—	—	—	—	—	—
	dr. 418						
SUB-TOTAL	cr. 128	546	208	354	147	—	354
CAPITAL CHARGES (see text)							
Depreciation	dr. 50						
Interest	39						
	dr. 89						
Profit	cr. 39						

At this level of profits, therefore, in both direct trade and cross-trade the:

Maximum net improvement in the balance of payments, as percentage of freight earnings, with the ship built wholly at home or received as a gift is

$$\frac{(546-354)}{546} \times 100 = 35\cdot2\,\%.$$

Minimum net improvement in the balance of payments as percentage of freight earnings, with the ship built abroad and paid for over ship's life at 6% is

$$\left[\frac{546-(354+50+39)}{546}\right] \times 100 = 18\cdot9\,\%.$$

N.B. Figures may not add to totals, nor assumptions appear to be precisely followed, because of rounding.

TABLE 3.2. *The balance of payments effects, in the average year of the ship's life, of substituting a national for a foreign ship* (when shipping is **unprofitable**).

(a) In a *direct trade*, and (b) in a *cross-trade*

(£000s p.a.)

Item (1)	Ship account (2)	Gains (3)	Losses by increased spending (4)		Losses by non-receipt (5)		Total (6)
(a) and (b)	(a) and (b)	(a) and (b)	(a)	(b)	(a)	(b)	(a) and (b)
REVENUE (freight)	cr. 464	464					
COSTS:							
Commissions at 5%	dr. 23		12	23	12	—	23
Stevedoring (as in Table 3.1)	136		68	136	68	—	136
Bunkers	28		28	28	—	—	28
Canal tolls	13		13	13	—	—	13
Port charges	50		25	50	25	—	50
(£ per day)							
Wages 150	55		5	11	5	—	11
Provisions 21	8		4	8	4	—	8
Stores 30	11		5	11	5	—	11
Repairs 125	46		23	46	23	—	46
Insurance 55	20		20	20	—	—	20
Sundries	4		2	4	2	—	4
Management	20		—	—	—	—	—
	dr. 414						
SUB-TOTAL		464	205	350	144	—	350
CAPITAL CHARGES	cr. 50						
(see text)							
Depreciation	dr. 50						
	dr. 50						
Profit	—						

At this level of profits, therefore, in both direct trade and cross-trade the:

Maximum net improvement in the balance of payments, as percentage of freight earnings, with the ship built wholly at home or received as a gift is

$$\frac{(464-350)}{464} \times 100 = 24\cdot 6\ \%.$$

Minimum net improvement in the balance of payments as percentage of freight earnings, with the ship built abroad and paid for over ship's life at 6 % is

$$\left[\frac{464-(350+50+39)}{464}\right] \times 100 = 5\cdot 4\ \%.$$

N.B. Figures may not add to totals, nor assumptions appear to be precisely followed because of rounding.

TABLE 3.3. *Percentages of gross earnings remaining as net improvements to the balance of payments when a national ship replaces a foreign one*

(Direct and cross-trades.)

As in Table	When shipping is		Maximum (%)	Minimum (%)
3.1 (*a*)	Profitable	{Direct trade	35·2	18·9
(*b*)		{Cross-trade	35·2	18·9
3.2 (*a*)	Unprofitable	{Direct trade	24·6	5·4
(*b*)		{Cross-trade	24·6	5·4

For this reason, Table 3.2 shows the position with net earnings sufficient only to cover depreciation. This is equivalent to gross profits of £5·0 per g.r.t. per year.

These tables show that, other things being equal, there is no difference between the net balance of payments effects of direct trades and cross-trades. The results are summarized above in Table 3.3.

Differences in national costs and efficiencies can be inserted in tables constructed on this pattern. The most important involve differences in earning power (because the earnings of a cargo line depend partly upon its reputation, e.g. for reliability and care in handling cargo, and also upon the frequency of service offered) and are extremely difficult to estimate. Others involve differences in factor prices and efficiencies. Thus, for example, wage costs depend partly on the levels of earnings and partly on the manning scale adopted or enforced by law or by agreement between employers and trade unions. Taking both of these into account the ratio of wage costs for USA ships to British ships is probably about 4.[1] For Australia the ratio may be in the region of 2·3.[2] In practice, and particularly with crew costs, the insertion of even such ratios as these does not make very much difference to the answer obtained.

[1] See e.g. Ferguson *et al.*, *op. cit.*, Table IV-7, and Sturmey, *op. cit.* p. 314.
[2] Calculated from Capt. J. P. Williams: 'The problems facing Australian shipping in the next decade', unpublished paper delivered to the Economic Society of Australia and New Zealand (Melbourne, April 1960), Table 6.

4

ECONOMIC CRITERIA FOR OPTIMAL SHIP DESIGNS

1. Introduction

There are generally several different ways of designing a ship; all of them may be safe and technically feasible but it is likely that one will be better than the others. Not only do we have many different types of engine and hull shapes to choose from, but any given flow of cargo can be carried in ships of different sizes and numbers, offering different service frequencies and, possibly, different sea speeds and turnround times. In addition to these fundamental elements of ship designs there are many minor decisions: should one have derricks or cranes, and in what numbers? Should one have this or that automatic or self-recording device? Or should one have none at all?

This paper is not concerned with the economics of these variations as such. It is not my purpose to discuss whether ships should be large or small, or fast or slow, or fitted with any particular piece of equipment. My purpose is the much more elemental (as distinct from elementary) one of offering a criterion which takes all aspects of the alternative designs into account and by which they may be compared. Moreover, it so happens that the criterion advocated in this paper is suitable, not only for determining which, of two or more designs, should be selected, but whether any of them should be built at all; and, if so, whether construction should be started now or postponed until some future date. This criterion, however, is not applicable to warships nor to any craft which do not, however indirectly, serve any commercial purpose. It is applicable to tramps, liners, tankers, coasters and specialized ships of all kinds; with some difficulty it can also be applied to those necessary vessels, like dredgers and other public service craft, which may not earn money for their owners, but which permit other ships to earn money for theirs.

This paper, then, is analytical rather than quantitative in nature. Practical experience of ship design, construction and operation, suitably adjusted to take account of likely developments and changes in the future, as well as the results of experiments (e.g. in ship model tanks and in cargo-handling gear), are all necessary ingredients in the application of the methods outlined here to any particular situation; you cannot do without them. No shipowner, shipbuilder or naval architect will, therefore, find in this paper ready-made answers to any of his immediate problems. Instead, they will find a method for producing the answers to some of those problems. And those problems, I suggest, are amongst the most important that they have.

There is, I believe, little in this paper which is fundamentally new to a professional economist familiar with recent work in the field of general investment criteria. (The list of references indicates the number of authors whose works I have plundered.) All I have done is to apply economic theory developed elsewhere (notably in the economics of water supply) to the peculiar circumstances of merchant shipping and to consider the implications. These circumstances raise a few points of some interest to economists, but the practical interest is limited to those connected with shipping and shipbuilding.

Thus, the questions for which this paper attempts to provide a methodology of answering are:

(1) Why build this ship at all?
(2) Why build it like this?
(3) Why build it now?

The first and the last of these may not be within the naval architect's professional sphere. These are included here because they are interesting questions and because, as noted above, they can be answered by precisely the same techniques as are described below.

2. Previous works

Although advice on the suitability of different ship designs is undoubtedly one of the functions of the naval architect, neither the basic textbooks of the subject nor the periodical literature normally available to practising workers in this field appear to give very much guidance. Thus, K. C. Barnaby[1] does not mention the subject of overall comparisons between different ship designs, intended for the same purposes, at all and discusses the different aspects of ship design

---

[1] *Basic naval architecture* (Hutchinson, 1963), 4th ed.

quite separately. The same could be said of Rossell and Chapman.[1] Attwood and Pengelly[2] say: 'In the early stages of a design the naval architect frequently has to proceed independently in trying alternatives for the same result...'; though nowhere do they say what criteria these trials should employ, nor in what terms they should be conducted.

This, of course, is not to suggest that no one has ever thought or written about the economics of ship design (and it is the economic comparison of designs that the commercial shipowner is interested in). Many people have done so[3] but, remarkably, the fact remains

---

[1] *Principles of naval architecture*, 2 vols. S.N.A.M.E. 1939 (currently under revision).

[2] *Theoretical naval architecture* (Longmans Green & Co., 1943).

[3] The principal published works were: W. C. Bergius: 'On the commercial economy of several types of merchant steamers and on some of the principal lines of steamship traffic', *Trans. I.N.A.* (1871); J. Hamilton: 'The speed and form of steamships considered in relation to length of voyage', *Trans. I.N.A.* (1883); J. Anderson: 'The most suitable sizes and speeds for general cargo steamers', *Trans. I.N.A.* (1918); E. Saxton White: 'The relationship between residuary resistance horse-power and forms of vessels', *Trans. N.E.C.I.E.S.* (1911–12); A. Urwin: 'The economic efficiency of merchant ships', *Trans. N.E.C.I.E.S.* (1918–19); G. S. Baker and J. L. Kent: 'Speed, dimensions and form of cargo vessels', *Trans. Inst. E. & S. in Scotland* (1918); A. C. J. Robertson: 'Economical cargo ships', *Trans. SNAME* (1919); J. Anderson: 'Further notes on the dimensions of cargo steamers', *Trans. I.N.A.* (1920); J. Tutin: 'The economic efficiency of merchant ships', *Trans. I.N.A.* (1922); Shotaro Kojima: 'The effects of shipping competition on freight rates', *Kyoto Univ. Econ. Rev.* (1927); Sir J. H. Biles: 'The draught and dimensions of the most economical ship', *Trans. I.N.A.* (1931); G. S. Baker: *Ship efficiency and economy*, Birchall (1942); W. MacGillivray: 'Speed at sea and despatch in port', *Trans. I.N.A.* (1948); G. S. Baker: *Ship design, resistance and screw propulsion*, Birchall (1949); E. V. Telfer: 'Economic speed trends', *Trans. SNAME* (1951); J. E. Church: 'Marine machinery of the immediate future from the shipowners point of view', *Trans. I Mar.E.* (1955); E. C. B. Corlett: 'On design of economic tramp ships', *Trans. I.N.A.* (1956); H. Benford: 'Engineering economy in tanker design', *Trans. SNAME* (1957); A. Strømme Svendsen, *Sea transport and shipping economics. Weltschiffahrts-Archiv* (Bremen, 1958); A. Strømme Svendsen: 'Factors determining the laying-up of ships', *Shipbuilding and shipping record*, 19 June 1958; H. Benford: 'Ocean ore carrier economics and preliminary design', *Trans. SNAME* (1958); H. Gripaios: *Tramp shipping* (Nelson, 1959); R. S. Neilsen: *Oil tanker economics*, Bremen, 1959; T. Thorburn: *Supply and demand for water transport* (Stockholm School of Economics, 1960); A. R. Ferguson *et al.*: *The economic value of the US merchant marine*, The Transportation Center, Northwestern University (Illinois, 1961); R. M. Elden: *Ship management: a study in definition and measurement* (Cornell Maritime Press, 1962); H. Benford, K. C. Thornton and E. B. Williams: 'Current trends in the design of iron-ore ships', *Trans. SNAME* (1962); S. G. Sturmey: *British shipping and world competition*

that few of them provide or discuss (except by implication) what the criteria for comparing ship designs should be. And of those who imply or advocate specific criteria there is none [with the notable exception of Professor Benford, whose paper this one partially overlaps] who employ the quite simple techniques discussed here. There are, however, a number of published works in engineering economy which advocate and describe these techniques: of these, the best-known is perhaps that by Grant and Ireson.[1] Professor Grant, however, makes no mention of shipping.

There is neither space, time, nor a great deal of point in summarizing all these references. There is, perhaps, some point in remarking that speed, size, powering, hull form and ratios of dwt./displacement or bale-cubic/dwt. are all so closely interrelated that it is impossible to achieve optimal levels of any one of them independently of the others. What we must optimize, therefore, is the design of the ship as a whole and, indeed, there are occasions, as Dr D. J. Doust has pointed out[2], when it is necessary to optimize the system within which the ship is intended to work.

A remarkable attempt to produce a criterion for measuring the economic efficiency of ships was produced in papers delivered to The Institution of Engineers and Shipbuilders in Scotland in 1918 by Messrs G. S. Baker and J. L. Kent[3] and to The Institution of Naval Architects (as it then was) in 1922 by Dr J. Tutin[4] (see Appendix 1). Their formulae, and those produced by various other authors, are, I think, open to several objections.

(Athlone Press, 1962); H. Benford: 'Influence of ship size and speed in cost of ocean bulk transportation', *International marine design and equipment* (Tothill Press, 1963); R. T. Crake: 'Long distance container economics', *ICHCA Quarterly Journal* (January 1963); Sir Stewart MacTier: 'Deep sea cargo liner design—a commercial reassessment', *Trans. R.I.N.A.* (1963); H. Benford: 'Principles of engineering economy in ship design', *Trans. SNAME* (1963); S. G. Sturmey: 'Some aspects of ocean liner economics' (Manchester Statistical Society, 1964); A. G. Hopper, P. H. Judd and G. Williams: 'Cargo handling and its effect on dry cargo ship design', *Trans. R.I.N.A.* (1964); D. J. Doust: 'The relative importance of trawler design to fishing economics as a whole' N.P.L. Ship Division Report No. 57 presented to FAO meetings on business decisions in fishery industries. Rome. (21–25 September 1964.)

[1] *Principles of engineering economy* (The Ronald Press Co., New York, 1960), 4th ed.   [2] *The relative importance of trawler design*, cit.
[3] *Speed dimensions and form of cargo vessels*, art. cit.
[4] *The economic efficiency of merchant ships*, art. cit.

First, they assume that a ship will have a constant distribution of costs and revenues through time. Partly because of the quadrennial classification surveys and partly because of the uneven incidence of tax allowances and the lag in tax collection in the United Kingdom this is quite unrealistic. The significance of this error will become apparent later in this paper.

Secondly, they produce their ratios with the first cost of the ship as the denominator of their fundamental equation; and this is assumed to hold good throughout the ship's life. But because the value of the ship falls as she gets older (and depreciation funds can be used to repay loans) the *average* capital employed is roughly half the initial cost. The Baker–Tutin formula, therefore, approximately halves the true rate of return. Clearly, this matters a great deal when the rate of return expected from a ship is compared with the rate of interest at which she is to be financed.

Thirdly, their formulae employ or assume simple mathematical relationships which, as was pointed out during the discussion on Dr Tutin's paper, are not necessarily of universal validity.

Fourthly, the formulae assume continuities in these relationships which are not necessarily valid either. Discontinuities in the relationships found in ship design are quite common. They are found, for example, in the speed/powering, relationship when the number of propellers is changed; and in the cargo capacity/cargo handling function when the number of hatches is changed. Nor can these discontinuities be built into any such formula because their quantitative effects depend on design details.

Fifthly, the formulae omit many of the relationships between variables. Thus, while fuel consumption is taken to be related to IHP and the relationship is built into the formulae, neither is explicitly related to the first cost of the vessel. Indeed, the formulae show no relationship between first cost and anything else except the annual bill for wages, insurance, etc., which is assumed to be proportionate. Assumptions like the last may sometimes be necessary in arriving at first approximations. They are politely referred to amongst economists as 'heroic'.

Finally, and most important of all, the answer is produced as a rate of return, or yield. But, since a smaller rate of return on a larger

5   G S I

capital may be more valuable than a larger rate of return on a smaller capital (I would rather have 10 % on £1,000,000 than 50 % on £1,000 if both were at the same degree of risk and the market cost of capital was 6 %), a simple rate of return is not necessarily a valid method of comparing alternative ways of doing the same thing. (If they were not mutually exclusive and both yields were free from risk and greater than the cost of borrowing we might emulate Winnie-the-Pooh and ask for both; but this is not the problem we are dealing with here.) It is also true that, where the capital sums involved and the rates of return are both the same, different economic lives may produce differing degrees of attractiveness—I would rather have 10 % on £1,000,000 for 20 years than for 10 years.

3. Economics

But Baker, Kent, Tutin and others were completely right in placing their emphasis on economic arguments and in measuring these in £ *s. d.* There is, indeed, no other way in which they can be measured. They were also correct in emphasizing profits as the criterion. This is because, except for owners of naval and public service craft, shipowners are in business to make profits. If they do not succeed in doing so, or if they ever give up trying to make profits, then, in the last resort, they will be unable either to maintain their capital intact or to raise fresh capital for expansion: they will go out of business. Moreover, if the directors and managers do not in fact dispose of the resources available to them in the most profitable way then they may be faced with either a shareholders' revolt or, more likely, a takeover bid. Either way they will lose their jobs. In the rest of this paper I shall assume that the shipowner is interested in maximizing his profits and that, therefore, he is interested in the most profitable ship design.

In countries where state, or state supported, shipowners exist the fleets may be operated with other objectives. One of the commonest of these is the improvement of the balance of payments. This is not as simple an objective as may appear at first sight for it is necessary to take into account not only the earnings of the ship, whether received in foreign exchange or not, and the overseas expenditure of the national ships, but also the expenditure within the country concerned of the foreign ships which they replace and any capital charges payable overseas. A description of the analysis required and a method of comparing projects designed to assist the balance of payments will be found above on pp. 46–60.

Economists have generally discussed the optimal methods of production in terms of the absolute levels of what they term 'factors of production' and in terms of the ratios between factors of production. These factors of production comprise anything that is used in any process of production, whether it is goods, like corn, that are being produced or services, like transporting by sea: they are usually classified as land, labour, capital and enterprise, though the economists' definition of land as 'the gifts of nature' clearly includes the sea! For purposes of exposition these factors of production, which may be sub-divided as often as you please, are necessarily regarded as being homogeneous.

But there have been three reasons why, until fairly recent years, the approach of the professional economist has been unsuitable for practical application by those concerned with the design of ships.

(1) The phrase 'maximization of profits' is ambiguous. Every businessman knows that the faster he gets his profits the better. He is not, therefore, indifferent between profits one year hence and ten years hence. But how are the two related?

(2) The economist was generally more interested in the optimal distribution of a community's resources between the various purposes to which they might be put (i.e. the problem of economic welfare) than in the problems of investment criteria for the businessman. This is largely because, until recent years, practical businessmen rarely asked economists to take an interest in such matters.

(3) The economist usually employed the marginal analysis; that is to say an analysis stated in terms of very small increments in the ratios between these supposedly homogeneous factors of production. But, where several factors of production are concerned (i.e. where each of the broad classifications mentioned above must be subdivided), this approach involves a very large number of design studies. Although indiarubber may be cheap, the time of naval architects is not; and delay in the construction of a ship may be even more expensive. However logical this approach may be it is inherently unsuitable for the

naval architect or shipowner because, in concentrating attention on optimizing ratios between factors of production, it draws attention away from optimizing techniques; and it is this question of optimal techniques which is the essence of naval architecture. Moreover, one of the most important factors of production in shipping is capital; that is, the ship herself. To put it mildly, there are considerable logical and conceptual difficulties involved in assuming capital to be homogeneous, especially when it is embodied in a ship.

Even, therefore, if naval architects had studied the elementary textbooks of economics (and it is surely unreasonable to have expected them to go further than the elementary works of a discipline that is not their own), it is very probable that they would not have found them to be of very much use. The criterion advocated in the next section of this paper in no way contradicts the marginal technique, but is not open to any of the objections stated above; it can be applied to any number of design studies, large or small, including different ways of financing the ship, and different dates of building. It is, in other words, capable of answering the three questions stated in the introduction: Should we build at all? If so, to what design? And when should we build?

4. A criterion for optimizing ship designs

Any criterion for determining the optimum investment for performing any given function involves estimating the answers to several questions. Essentially, these are no more than enquiries as to the extent to which things will be different as a result of the investment. Thus, in the context of ships, we are concerned with the following:

(1) What will be the gross benefits over the ship's life? In the simplest case this is the gross earnings of the ship; indeed, with many ship types the question is just that. But where the ship is operating as part of a liner service then there may be some effects on the earnings of other ships in the same ownership and these must be taken into account. Either way, the figure we need is the difference between what the revenue would be with the investment and what it would have been without it.

(2) What is the cost of the ship? This can be divided into two parts: (*a*) Initial cost, conventionally referred to as the capital cost though it

may include some elements which an accountant would not normally recognize as capital (e.g. any special training that may be required by the crew, or the cost of having senior officers standing by during the building period). It is not, therefore, necessarily quite the same as the contract price agreed between the builder and the owner, even if we leave items like owner's stores out of account. (*b*) The continuing costs of the ship. Often, these are referred to as operating or running costs, though some, like the increase in management costs and commissions to brokers, may be external to the ship. Mostly, however, they can be divided into the familiar accounting headings of fuel, wages, stores, port charges, and so forth. [But see R. M. Elden's study[1] for a discussion of whether this is the most useful division.] Because capital cost has been included in 2 (*a*) it would be double-counting to include any part of depreciation under this heading.

(3) What is the life of the ship, either to scrapping or to sale second-hand? This will depend largely on the physical characteristics of the ship (anti-corrosion precautions, possibly), the work she has to undertake and the policies of the owners. Because second-hand values are usually based on the estimated profitability of the remaining ship's life, policies preferring one to the other will not make very much difference to the final answer except where the ship is highly specialized. But, since the second-hand sale of a highly specialized ship is unlikely, we may conveniently assume that all ships are retained until scrapping.

(4) What is the distribution of estimated revenues over the estimated life? In the years of the quadrennial classification surveys (at least for the later ones) the ship will be out of service and for increasing periods. In those years, therefore, her earnings will be reduced. We can *not* assume that the distribution of earnings throughout the ship's life will be constant. In addition, any rising or falling trend in the supply-demand position of the type of ship under consideration may affect the freight rate at which she trades and, if she is a liner, the load factor at which she operates.

(5) What is the distribution of the estimated operating costs over the estimated life? Again, because of the quadrennial surveys these

---

[1] *Ship management: a study in definition and measurement* (Cornell Maritime Press, 1962).

costs will be greater in some years than in others. Again, there may be rising or falling trends in the costs of operation. The methods by which such trends may be brought into the calculation are described in the next section.

(6) What is the scrap (or second-hand) value at the end of the ship's life? Because scrap values are easier to estimate than second-hand values this is a further reason for assuming that the ship will be retained in the same ownership until scrapping.

The answers to all these questions can be stated in terms of time and money. We can, therefore, draw up a table (a worked example is given in Appendix 2) in which each line represents a year of the ship's life. The first line represents the year of construction. In column 1 we can place all the earnings of the ship; these we may regard as positive components of cash flow, because they are the money gained by having the ship in those years. In column 2 we can place all the costs of the ship, capital and operating, against the years in which they are paid. (It is the cash movements that we are estimating; costs must, therefore, be entered in the years of payment, not that in which they were incurred. This is particularly important where tax payments are concerned—another topic which is dealt with in the next section.)

By subtracting column 2 from column 1 we arrive at column 3: 'net cash flow', for each year in which receipts and payments caused by the ship will take place. In some years, almost certainly the year of construction, and very likely the later quadrennial survey years, this figure will be negative. In the rest it should be positive if the ship has any chance of being an economic proposition. We have now summarized the answers to all the questions stated earlier in this section into a single column of figures. It remains to relate them to one another. This can be done by recognizing that the present value of a sum of money accruing in the future is less than that of an equal sum of money accruing now.

This is for two reasons, both of which are necessary. First it seems to be a built-in characteristic of the majority of people that they value a future receipt at less than a current one of equal size and risk. This attitude is known as 'discounting the future'. Because common observation shows us that different people discount the future at different rates (children, for example, appear to discount the future at very high rates), and because there is no meaningful method of averaging available to us, this argument will not tell us at what rate we ought to discount time when acting on behalf of a shipowner. (Though one could try asking the shipowner.) It merely tells us that we ought to do it somehow.

Secondly, capital is productive; that is to say, it can be invested so as to produce a return at intervals without diminishing itself. Moreover, in a developed society capital does not have to be embodied directly in physical form in order to earn a return. It can be invested in any of an extremely wide variety of paper assets with varying levels of return and risk and with varying provisions for repayment of capital. Repayment can often be obtained before the arranged date by selling the asset to someone else; it is to facilitate such sales that the Stock Exchange and money markets exist. In spite of the fact that, at any given time, different current returns exist (we can trace most of these to differing degrees of risk, different repayment provisions and different expectations of future returns—what the investment analyst means by 'growth prospects') we can observe these rates and obtain evidence of what rate we ought to use. The subject is further discussed in the next section. We will now assume that we have a rate of discount.

The best-known formula for calculating compound interest is:

$$P_n = P_o(1+r)^i,$$

where P_n is the sum produced after i years,

P_o is the sum now, and

r is the annual rate of interest expressed as a decimal.

From this it follows that:

$$\frac{P_o}{P_n} = \frac{1}{(1+r)^i} = (1+r)^{-i}.$$

In other words, for every £1 accruing in the future the equivalent present value is £$(1+r)^{-i}$. In order to find the present value of any future sum we multiply it by this. Values of $(1+r)^{-i}$, known as discount factors, may be obtained, for any reasonable range of values of r and i, from financial tables.

We can now add a fourth column of discount factors for our given values of r and i, multiply these by the net cash flow figures in the third column and place the result in a fifth column, 'discounted cash flow'. Where the net cash flow figures were negative, the equivalent figures in this fifth column must also be negative. We then sum the column algebraically. The total, which is termed the 'net present value' (NPV) of the investment, can be expressed mathematically as:

$$\text{NPV} = \sum_{i=0}^{i=n} A_i(1+r)^{-i}$$

where A_i is the net cash flow for year i and n is the number of years in the ship's life.

Where the initial cost is to be paid off in a single lump sum then it will be discounted (to date of payment) by a factor of precisely 1·00000. An alternative, therefore, is to omit the initial cost line of the table, proceed as described above and subtract the initial cost from the sum of the fifth column. If this is done then the formula becomes:

$$\text{NPV} = \left[\sum_{i=1}^{i=n} A_i(1+r)^{-i}\right] - C,$$

where C is the initial cost. This is the formula employed in Appendix 2.

The answers to all the questions specified earlier in this section have now been summarized into a single figure of net present value. This figure may be compared with the net present value of any other project. For this purpose, 'other projects' include different ship designs, different ways of financing the same design and different dates of commencing construction. The different designs may be part of a series, e.g. of variations in size or speed, or they may be totally unrelated to one another.

The different ways of financing the design may well include some with deferred payments and interest charges. Where this is so, and subject to any adjustments such as are described in the next section in respect of a changing general price-level, all such payments may be included, as and when they are expected to occur, in the negative cash flow column. It may then happen that none of the early years of the ship's life have any negative net cash flows at all.

Net present value may be either positive or negative. If it is negative on all the projects being considered then either too high a discount rate has been employed or none of them should be 'undertaken.

If only one project has a positive net present value then it should be undertaken. If more than one project has a net positive present value then the one with the greatest net present value should be chosen.

Subject to the difficulties mentioned in section 5 below we have thus arrived at a clear and unambiguous rule for answering the three questions quoted in the introduction. We should build the ship because it has a positive net present value; we should build this design because it has a greater net present value than any other; and we should build it at this time because its net present value is greater than if it were built at any other time. This method is open to none of the objections levelled above at the Baker–Tutin formula, but it is accompanied by a number of difficulties, some of which may safely be ignored and some of which must be faced and overcome. The theory and practice of net present value, and of investment criteria generally, has been widely discussed.[1] The study by Merrett and Sykes[2] is particularly recommended in this context.

5. Practical difficulties

Although most of the difficulties described in this section are concerned with providing the answers to the questions posed at the beginning of the previous section, it must be emphasized that the net present value criterion is not alone in requiring the information. Much the same information is required for any other method of comparing ship designs in economic terms. In particular, it may be noted

[1] W. H. White: 'The rate of interest, the marginal efficiency of capital and investment programming', *Economic Journal* (1958); J. F. Wright: 'The marginal efficiency of capital', *Economic Journal* (December 1959); C. S. Soper: 'The marginal efficiency of capital: a further note', *Economic Journal* (March 1959); P. Massé: *Optimal Investment Decisions* (Prentice-Hall, USA, 1962); Hirschleifer, de Haven and Milliman: *Water supply: Economics, technology and policy* (Chicago, 1960); H. Bierman, Jr and S. Smidt: *The capital budgeting decision* (Macmillan, New York, 1960); D. L. Munby: 'Investment in road and rail transport', *Journal of the Institute of Transport* (March 1962); R. Turvey: 'Present value versus internal rate of return; an essay in the theory of the third best', *Economic Journal*, March 1963; A. M. Alfred: 'Discounted cash flow— the proper assessment of investment projects', *The Investment Analyst* (December 1963); C. D. Foster and M. E. Beesley: 'Estimating the social benefit of constructing an underground railway in London, *Journal of the Royal Statistical Society* (1963).

[2] *The finance and analysis of capital projects* (Longmans, 1963).

that the practice of averaging revenues and operating costs, especially repair costs, over the life of the ship is, in general, as likely to lead to wrong answers as the use of purely historical information, unadjusted for likely future changes upon which Mr R. B. Monteath has so strongly commented.[1]

The remaining difficulties may now be discussed.

(a) CHANGING PRICES IN GENERAL
(i.e. the changing value of money)

Although annual accounts drawn up on a historic cost basis may show a gradually changing annual profit on a ship (increasing if the value of money is falling) after depreciation and interest charges, if any, this is not necessarily a changing profit in terms of purchasing power. In real terms, the change may be quite spurious if capital is not being maintained intact in real terms. With few exceptions it is neither necessary nor desirable to make any allowances for changes in the value of money in either the positive or the negative cash flow columns. Amongst these exceptions are the following: when the ship is financed on fixed interest terms; as, for example, when the contract with the shipbuilder involves deferred payments specified in money terms; when the revenue is derived in fixed money terms, e.g. from a long term charter without escalation provision; the tax allowances, particularly those for depreciation and, possibly, the balancing charge (see subsection d). If prices in general are rising then the real value of these will be declining. Before they are inserted into the cash flow columns, therefore, these sums should be adjusted by the proportionate extent to which it is estimated that prices will have changed between the base year to which all cash flows are being discounted and the date on which the payments concerned are due to be made.

(b) CHANGING RELATIVE PRICES

Whether the value of money is changing or not it is common for prices to move relative to one another. (It is because of this that we measure changes in the value of money by index-numbers and it is for the same reason that we may get different answers if we employ dif-

---

[1] The effect of modern cargo handling methods on the design of ships and ports, *ICHCA Quarterly Journal* (October 1964).

ferent weights.) Changing relative prices must be allowed for. Probably the simplest way to do this is to take the expected rate of change of the price of each factor of production (e.g. stevedores' wages, seamens' wages, oil fuel, etc.), relative to the expected rate of change of prices in general. Thus, if we expect prices in general to rise at 2 % p.a. and we expect the price of oil fuel to stay the same, we must calculate as if we expected the price of oil fuel to fall by 2 % p.a. Given a rising real national income it is very likely that there will be relative price changes. In particular wages will be likely to rise faster than prices in general.

(c) CHANGES IN PRODUCTIVITY

If a factor of production becomes more effective then one may be able to achieve the same result by using less of it. Unless, therefore, its price is rising relatively to other prices at exactly the same rate (an unlikely coincidence) we must allow for this. But, in practice, it is unlikely that we can make any such allowance and for two reasons. First, the effectiveness of a factor of production in, or around, a ship is largely determined by the design of that ship. Once you have built a ship intended to be operated by a given number of crew it is quite difficult to change either the number of men or the proportions of the various grades. Similarly, once the engine has been built it is quite difficult to improve its specific fuel consumption.

Secondly, even if it is possible to make such alterations, it is rather unlikely that we would know about them now *and* be unable to use the improvements now. How, for example, are we to estimate that in five years' time someone will invent a perpetual anti-fouling paint? If such a paint existed we could use it now: if it does not exist now then it is rather unlikely that we can estimate its future advent. However, if we can make such estimates, e.g. in respect of port development, so much the better.

(d) TAXATION

Shipowners do not operate ships in order to earn money for their governments: they do so in order to earn money for themselves and for their shareholders. We must, therefore, calculate our net cash flows after tax. This may be difficult and it is tempting not to do it at all. But taxation is very important in this age and to omit it would be to falsify the picture. Nor can one assume that, because many British shipping companies have in recent years earned such small profits that they have had no taxable incomes and therefore no tax bills, that one may legitimately ignore tax altogether.

Not only is tax important as such, but so are the various allowances which may be made against taxable income. In respect of ships these are, in the United Kingdom, very significant indeed, consisting as they do of an investment allowance of 40 % of the capital cost of the ship, and depreciation allowances of 15 % on the reducing balance system. Such allowances have the effect of making capital cheaper and weighting our calculations in favour of ships with high capital costs and correspondingly low operating costs; thus there is no question but that they can have significant effects on the optimum ship design. Professor Merrett and Mr Sykes have published a simple and ingenious system of incorporating these allowances into a present value calculation.[1] Their table includes a column applicable to ships. Unfortunately, this system is strictly appropriate only where the distribution of net cash flows over the life of the ship is fairly flat. We have already seen that this is not so.

The only way to tackle this problem thoroughly, therefore, is to work right through, using the tax allowances and the appropriate rates of tax. In this connection it is important to remember that in the United Kingdom (but not in some other countries, e.g. the USA) companies actually pay their tax bills some considerable time after they have earned the profits concerned. Commonly the delay is of the order of 1–2 years and this, like any other postponement of payments without a credit charge, is valuable to the debtor.

(*e*) THE APPROPRIATE RATE OF DISCOUNT

The cost of using capital (or, indeed, of using anything else) for one purpose lies in not being able to use it for the next best alternative purpose. This concept is known to economists as 'opportunity cost'. To find, therefore, the rate of discount applicable to ships we must discover the rate of return which could have been obtained, not in the average alternative use, but in the best alternative use. This will vary

---

[1] *Finance and analysis of capital projects*, p. 56.

from time to time and, possibly, from place to place. The appropriate rate of discount for 1965 is not the same as that for 1935; that for the United Kingdom may not be the appropriate one for India or for the USA.

It is tempting, but quite wrong, to say that one can now borrow on fixed interest terms at about x % and that this is good enough. First, this rate may, or may not, take due account of any prospects that may exist for changing values of money. Secondly, under United Kingdom tax law payments of fixed interests are deductible before taxable income is arrived at. Thirdly, there are many different ways of borrowing, and of lending, money with different rates attached to each. Nor can one take either the dividend or the earnings yields on stocks and shares, for these vary considerably between different securities.

A recent study,[1] suggests that, taking capital gains, dividends and tax into account, the yield on unit trusts (in the USA these are called open-ended mutual funds) in the post-war years has been 11·6 %. Allowance for rising prices would bring this down to about 8 %. Merrett and Sykes therefore suggest that it is hard to rate the opportunity cost of capital below 7–8 % in real terms and after tax, especially when it is borne in mind that governmental policies emphasize stable growth for the future.

But A. M. Alfred has produced a different answer and without extrapolating historical trends.[2] To a yield on the *Financial Times*— Actuaries 500 shares index of 2·8 % net of tax the author adds $3\frac{1}{2}$ % for the growth of the economy, subtracts 1 % for the remuneration of new capital and calculates a yield on this basis of 5·3 %. To this he adds 0·3 % for the gearing effect by which equity investors gain more than holders of fixed interest assets when profits increase without inflation and a further 0·2 % for the extra gain that they make with a moderate degree of inflation. He then suggests that he is prepared to compromise with Merrett and Sykes at 7 % as a prospective opportunity cost of capital after tax and in real terms. This, or some similar figure, remains the relevant figure for discounting to net present value

[1] The Consumers' Association Ltd.: 'Unit Trusts' *Which?* (May, 1963) commented on by Merrett and Sykes, *ibid.*

[2] *Discounted cash flow and corporate planning*, Woolwich Economic Paper No. 3 (1964).

because, even if we borrow at 6 % fixed interest terms, or say 2 % net of tax and in real terms, the shipping company is still under an obligation to do as well with these funds as typical equities. Otherwise the shareholders would be better off if the company invested its borrowings in equities and thus gradually turned itself into an investment trust.

(*f*)   UNCERTAINTY

No one can foretell the future precisely; everyone who has to consider whether to make an investment, how to make it, and when to make it has to try to do so. Generally, one examines what has been happening in the past, attempts to establish a trend and then considers whether, and if so to what extent, that trend is likely to be maintained in the future.

But there will inevitably be uncertainty attached to any such predictions. A partial answer to this problem lies in the fact that uncertainty is likely to be greater as the interval between the date of the prediction and the date in respect of which the prediction is made increases. Thus the discounting process will reduce the quantitative effects of errors as they tend to get larger. (The discount factor for 25 years at 7 % is only 0·184249.)

This, however, is not all we can say about techniques available to deal with the problem of uncertainty. We can work through our calculations taking, first, an optimistic but credible series of estimates, secondly, a pessimistic but equally credible series of estimates and, thirdly, an estimate which is neither optimistic nor pessimistic and which has the greatest credibility of all. This will not be the mean of the other two unless the relative probabilities, and their outcomes, are both normally distributed (or biased in opposite senses and to equivalent extents). The degrees of credibility should preferably be stated, since qualitative terms like 'reasonably optimistic' or 'fairly pessimistic' are ambiguous.

Extending this approach, we could make a number of estimates, three for each component of our calculations which is subject to a significant degree of uncertainty. The number of components is, in practice, likely to be so large and the number of possible combinations so much larger that, if the calculations are to be completed in time to be of any use, an electronic computer must be employed. This, however, should present little difficulty for, in the first place, computers are widely used in ship and shipyard calculations already and, in the second place, it is both simple and cheap to hire time on a commercial computer. Either of these methods is better than subsuming uncertainty in an arbitrary and unquantified manner into a necessarily arbitrary increase in the discount rate. To go, on the other hand, further in the employment of probabilities is almost certainly to be guilty of two faults: the first of these is spurious accuracy; the second is more fundamental.

For, even if we had sufficient information to calculate it, the actuarial value of an investment, taking account of all the probabilities involved, is not the same as its utility to a shipowner. The latter must take into account the particular shipowner's attitude to risk-bearing. For example, a shipowner who was cautious and averse to risk-bearing might prefer a project with a most credible yield of 8 % and a 95 % probability of being between 6 % and 10 % to one whose most likely yield was 10 % (on the same initial cost), but with a 95 % probability of being between 5 % and 15 %. Another, with a different attitude to risk-bearing, might rank these two alternatives in the opposite order.

Thus, although there is necessarily an element of uncertainty in our calculations, and even though it may be reduced by the discounting process, we can indicate its effects on the size of our criterion for answering the three questions posed in the introduction to this paper. Unless we can demonstrate that our best design has a positive net present value even on our pessimistic estimates this may have a crucial effect upon the answer to the first question: why should we build? But it is likely, on the whole, to have less effect on the answers to the other two: why build it this way? and why build it now? And it is the second of these three questions which is the real concern of naval architects. The first and the third questions are more the concern of the shipowners; their decisions will depend upon their judgment; for no one can tell a businessman how much risk he ought to be willing to bear, any more than one can tell him what he ought to have for lunch. And even for answering these two questions we have substantially reduced the area within which judgment has to operate.

(g) THE CHOICE OF BASE YEAR

Every project which is being discounted must be discounted to a base year. Every project which is being compared must be discounted to the same base year. It is a matter of convenience whether the base year is the present date, or the year of construction, or the first year of service, or whatever. If the base year is later than the first in which any cash flow exists as a result of this investment then the discounting formula must be adjusted so as to increase those cash flows, and for exactly the same reason that the cash flows subsequent to the base year will be reduced by the discounting formula.

(h) THE CHOICE OF END-YEAR OR CONTINUOUS CASH FLOWS

The formulae have been quoted in this paper as if the positive and negative cash flows occurred simultaneously and at the end of each twelve-monthly period. This is not a realistic representation for what actually happens in any shipping firm. But, provided that all projects being compared are treated alike, this is most unlikely to matter very much. In the first place, and although it may be possible to estimate the distribution of the earning of revenues and the incurring of costs within each year of ship's life (for example in a trade with known seasonal fluctuations), the distribution of actual receipts and payments may often be quite different and extremely difficult to estimate. The cost of calculating it, supposing it can be done at all, may well be greater than the benefits conferred on our calculations.

In the second place, the use of end-year cash flows may be justified on the grounds that, if we are employing calendar years, construction may not start at the beginning of a calendar year, and, if we are employing twelve-monthly periods starting with the commencement of construction, or the first capital payment, the use of end-year, instead of the more realistic mid-year cash flows, merely introduces a small element of caution into the calculations. What really matters is that all alternatives should be treated alike.

If anyone objects to having even a small element of caution built in to their methods of analysis a simple adjustment may be made which will substitute an assumption of mid-year for end-year cash flows. This adjustment consists of employing discount factors for $(i-1)$

instead of i and producing a net present value which is then discounted by $(1+r)^{-0.5}$ to obtain the true net present value on this
assumption. Generally this will make no significant difference either
to the answer in respect of any given design or to the comparison
between different designs. Indeed, if there were alternative designs so
closely matched that this adjustment affected the choice between
them it is highly probable that the decision ought really to be made
on technical, social, or aesthetic grounds.

(*i*) PUBLIC SERVICE CRAFT

For the purpose of this sub-section in term 'public service craft' is
defined as including all those vessels mentioned in the introduction as
not earning money for their owners, but operating so as to enable
other ships to earn money for theirs. The most obvious example is,
perhaps, the dredger, though some vessels which might fall in this
category, e.g. cable-layers and pilot vessels, do not necessarily work
wholly, or even mainly, in the confines of ports and harbours.

Where these craft are to be hired from contractors the problem of
optimal design is one for the contractor, not the hirer, and it can be
dealt with on the lines already discussed. Again, when craft owned or
operated by a port authority do earn money, e.g. tug hire, then the
same procedures may be applied. Alternatively, where craft are
required for important and occasional tasks, such as wreck removal
and salvage, the decision whether to have such a craft, and, if so,
what its design should be, may well be so dominated by technical
requirements that economic factors have little or no significance.

But where the craft is to be owned and operated by a public
authority and where there are choices available between different
technical solutions (e.g. in methods or rates of dredging or prime
mover) then economic factors can be significant. The problem is how
to make the optimal choice in the absence of positive components of
cash flow.

This problem can be solved in either of two ways. First, by the
application of cost-benefit analysis; which means that, since these
craft are conferring benefits on society, e.g. by enabling larger (or
more) ships to use a given port, these benefits should be quantified in
money terms and their totals treated as if they were the positive com-

ponents of cash flow. This is a long, difficult, and expensive process; since no calculation is worth making unless the benefits arising from it are greater than its cost the use of this technique is generally confined to very large and expensive projects. It has, for example, been used in studies on the London–Birmingham motorway,[1] on the Victoria Line underground railway for London,[2] and on the Channel Tunnel.[3] The complexity of any of these studies should convince the readers that such techniques are inappropriate for deciding the design of a dredger, however intellectually stimulating the work might be.

The second method is simpler and comes near to the techniques of minimizing cost which are generally in use in such situations. If we do not know the benefits and if it is not worth the considerable effort of estimating them, then we cannot know any mathematical relationship that may exist between benefits and the level or form of activity. For present purposes, therefore, I shall assume that it has already been decided that the activity should be undertaken, and to a prescribed extent. The problem that remains, therefore, is how to do it; and the answer is that it should be done in the cheapest way possible. But 'the cheapest way possible' involves taking account of factors 2, 3, 5 and 6, mentioned in the opening paragraph of Section 4.

We can then calculate the negative cash flows throughout the life of the vessel and their present value, using either of the formulae given above. The answer will, of course, be negative and, therefore, it must be minimized instead of being maximized. In other words, the best design for a vessel where benefits to society cannot, or have not, been calculated is the design with the smallest negative net present value.

(*j*) ALTERNATIVE DESIGNS WITH DIFFERING LIVES

Where alternative designs have differing lives, e.g. because of different corrosion rates, net present value is not a valid criterion because investments are not being compared over the same period of time. The shorter-lived alternative will involve earlier replacement and this

[1] T. M. Coburn, M. E. Beesley and D. J. Reynolds: *The London–Birmingham Motorway: Traffic and economics* (HMSO, 1960).
[2] C. D. Foster and M. E. Beesley: 'Estimating the social benefit of constructing an underground railway in London', *J. Roy. Statist. Soc.* (1963).
[3] *Proposals for a fixed channel link:* Joint Report by British and French Officials. Cmnd. 2137, HMSO (1963).

must be taken into account. Obviously, if all net cash flows (including initial costs) are identical for the alternative designs and their difference lies only in their life expectancies then the more durable one is the better. But a problem remains if net cash flows differ as well as the useful lives. If we fail to take account of this problem we shall bias our calculations in favour of the longer-lived design.

The problem may be overcome in any of three ways:

(1) Consider each design as if it were repeated up to the lowest common multiple of the lives. This is a cumbersome calculation and involves the additional disadvantage that, in a period when improvements in ship design may be expected, the replacement ship will probably be a better one; but it is almost impossible to say in what respects it will be better or how much the improvements will be worth.

(2) Use the incremental or differential yield method described in section 6. This, too, is laborious, especially when there are many alternatives and also when it is necessary to avoid the possibility of anomalous results by the 'extended yield method' also described in the next section.

(3) Calculate the net present values of the alternative designs as described in section 5 above and convert them into equivalent annuities extending over their respective useful lives. This may be done by employing the same rate of discount as was employed in the calculation of net present value and the appropriate financial tables. Thus, if we have a design with a life expectancy of 25 years and a net present value of £500,000 to compare with one having a life expectancy of 30 years and a net present value of £525,000, their relative attractiveness can be compared by looking up the 25-year annuity having a capitalized value of £500,000 at 7 % with the 30-year annuity having a capitalized value of £525,000 at 7 %. For these examples the figures are in fact £42,905 and £42,308 respectively. In this example, therefore, the shorter-lived design is the better, even though it has the smaller net present value.

The last of these three methods is by far the easier to calculate and has the additional recommendation (from the calculator's point of view) that it avoids predicting the rate of improvement in ship design. In principle, however, this is a disadvantage though it is probably one we can do nothing about.

6. Yield

It has already been noted that, for the comparison of projects (e.g. ship designs) which are mutually exclusive in that they are alternatives to one another, the simple comparison of percentages of profit to capital may be misleading; indeed it may even reverse the order of attractiveness. It is sometimes claimed that, if one is in any doubt as to the true cost of capital, the calculation of yield enables one to produce a figure which does not imply any specific cost. To my mind, however, this is dodging the issue; for the yield must be compared with something, and if not with the cost of capital then with what? Nevertheless, businessmen often wish to see such percentages and are accustomed to thinking in terms of them. There is, moreover, a technique (described below) which will enable mutually exclusive projects to be compared in terms of yield. When properly applied it will produce exactly the same answers as the net present value method; and it requires exactly the same information. The choice between the two methods is, therefore, largely a matter of personal preference.

In general, the percentage, or yield, on the best design may be calculated by solving either of the two formulae given earlier for r where net present value is zero. The result goes by various names, including rate of return, internal rate of return, marginal efficiency of capital and investor's method and has been used by financial analysts for centuries. (Professor Benford[1] gives it yet another name: equivalent interest rate of return.) Transposing the initial cost ('C') in the second formula given above enables us to see that this yield is the rate of return which discounts the future cash flows arising from the project to a sum equal to the initial cost. In other words, it is the maximum rate of interest at which the shipowner could finance his ship on normal (British) bank overdraft terms or any equivalent (i.e. where interest is charged only on the outstanding balance of the loan) in the absence of uncertainty.

In spite of the fact that yield, as such, does not provide a valid comparison of mutually exclusive projects this method can be used, though indirectly, for the comparison of ship designs by computing

[1] *Principles of engineering economy in ship design*, cit.

what is called the differential or incremental yield. This means that the net cash flows of the design with the lowest initial cost are subtracted from those of another, year by year, and a yield calculated on the difference between the two initial costs. If this yield is greater than the opportunity cost of capital then the more expensive design is the better.

As noted above, calculations of incremental yield will produce exactly the same results as net present value calculations. It is, however, laborious to calculate. So, for that matter, is an ordinary yield on a design with an uneven net cash flow pattern, since it has to be done by trial and error followed by interpolation to the first decimal place, if required. (Calculating to the second decimal place is spurious accuracy.)

A further possible disadvantage is that the incremental net cash flows are even more prone to contain negative figures than the net cash flows usually derived from ships. This can lead to multiple or absurd answers in certain circumstances. These anomalous situations are unlikely to arise *during* the life of the ship, for they do not occur every time that the net cash flow series contains negative figures subsequent to the first year. They only arise when the negative net cash flows are so large that the net present value at that point in the ship's life is itself negative (i.e. when they are not followed by positive cash flows sufficiently large to make net present value positive in the years of the negative cash flows). Clearly, the ship would, at that point in her life, be a liability and not an asset at all; she would then be scrapped. That is to say, her economic life would be at an end, no matter what her physical life expectancy might be.

These anomalous situations may, however, arise in the calculation of yields for ships because tax payments (in the United Kingdom) are normally made one or two years in arrears. That is to say, there may well be a negative cash flow, consisting of tax, in the year or so immediately after that in which the ship is scrapped. This need not lead to any anomaly: if it does the matter can be dealt with by reconstructing the time-series of net cash flows by discounting (at the cost of capital) the negative cash flow back to a year with positive cash flows sufficiently large to absorb it. We then have a time-series of net cash flows which is precisely equivalent to the original one, but which has no negative figure at the end. No risk of anomalous results will then exist and this time-series can be solved, as described above, so as to produce a yield or internal rate of return.

7. Conclusions

In this paper the criterion of net present value has been presented as valid for answering the three questions which must be answered, implicitly or explicitly, every time a shipowner considers building a ship: if it is positive for any design then building a ship to that design will be a better use of the resources involved than that which could reasonably be expected elsewhere; the design with the greatest net present value should be selected because it will be the most profitable, taking all economic factors into account; and if we estimate that net present value would be greater if we postponed construction, then that is what we should do. It has also been shown that, on this design, the yield, or internal rate of return, may be calculated. Thus, our principal criterion of net present value is cardinal; its reference point is the value of all the resources in their next best alternative use (not just that of capital); its unit is money value in current terms; the answer is expressed in terms of the extra sum of money which the shipowner should be willing to pay, over and above the initial cost of the ship, rather than do without it altogether. (He will, however, never be called upon actually to pay this extra sum, partly because of competition between shipbuilders and partly because of uncertainty.)

It is true that all this involves estimating the future in as precise a fashion as possible and that this involves uncertainty. While no one has any sort of magic wand with which to make uncertainty disappear, the effects of the degree of uncertainty in any particular component of the calculations, and in all of them together, can be estimated. In order to do so, however, the naval architect must make use of the judgments of many others. It is not sufficient for a naval architect to be given a number of absolute requirements for a design; his work must be integrated (whether permanently or on an *ad hoc* basis) with the whole of the rest of the organization and there must be adequate arrangements for feeding the required information and analysis in both directions. Neither the naval architect nor anyone else is required to be omniscient. He is merely required to do the best he can and to analyse the results in a rational manner; and any form of analysis other than net present value or the variation on yield discussed above is likely to produce the wrong answer. This, as Merrett and Sykes have shown,[1] is true of criteria involving pay-back periods, ratios of average profits before or after depreciation to first cost, or to average capital employed, and methods involving the inclusion of purely book-keeping transactions or positive or negative cash flows not related to the ship under consideration (such as the depreciation on pre-existing ships or arbitrary allocations of overhead costs). It is equally true of hunches, blind repetition of previously successful designs and decisions based on the allegedly overwhelming importance of unquantified factors.

None of this, however, is to decry, to any extent whatever, the virtues of practical experience. On the contrary, the whole of this paper could be re-stated by saying that past experience, and the more practical the better, must be systematically collected, properly analysed and then applied. Sometimes this may indicate the repetition of previous ideas, suitably modified to meet the changes continually taking place in the world around us. At other times and particularly, perhaps, in periods when traditional solutions are showing low profits, it may indicate radically different and technologically exciting solutions.

I have talked in terms of shipowners maximizing their profits. In practice, of course, no shipowner operates in a vacuum. If one shipowner obtains a more profitable design, so may all his competitors. The result of this is that the profits are shared with the consumers of sea transport through freight rates that are lower than they otherwise would have been, whether this takes the form of an actual reduction in freight rates or the postponement of an increase. And, if this is so, then the only hope for the shipowner who really wants to maximize his profits is to keep at least one jump ahead of his competitors, not now, but always.

Acknowledgements

I am indebted to various officials of HM Treasury, the Ministry of Transport and the National Ports Council for commenting on an

[1] *Finance and analysis of capital projects*, cit.

early draft of this paper. I am indebted to HM Treasury and the Ministry of Transport for permission to publish it and to the Royal Institution of Naval Architects for library services. I alone am responsible for the views expressed and for any errors and omissions.

APPENDIX 1

The Baker–Kent–Tutin formula is:

$$E = \frac{36500V[(f-t)C - xT - qklD^{\frac{2}{3}}LV^2]}{(L+n_LV)P} - 100y \ \%,$$

where

E = efficiency ($\%$);

C = cargo deadweight in tons;

T = net tonnage;

D = displacement tonnage;

P = first cost in £;

V = sea speed in nautical miles *per day*;

f = freight rate in £ per ton weight;

t = sum of brokerage, management and stevedoring in £ per ton;

x = tonnage dues in £ per net ton for complete voyage;

l = a factor given by IHP = $lD^{\frac{2}{3}}V^3$;

q = cost of fuel in £ per ton;

k = tons of fuel per day per IHP;

yP = sum of insurance, repairs, wages, depreciation in £;

L = length of voyage in miles;

n_L = number of days in port for loading, discharging, etc.

Then:

(1) $(f-t)C$ = earnings per voyage from cargo;

(2) xT = port dues per voyage;

(3) $qklD^{\frac{2}{3}}LV^2$ = cost of fuel per voyage;

(4) $\dfrac{365V}{L+n_LV}$ = number of such voyages p.a.

Equation (3) embodies, *inter alia*, the assumption that daily fuel consumption of a ship varies as the cube of the speed.

From these we get:

$$E = \frac{\dfrac{365V}{L+n_LV}[(f-t)C-xT-qklD^{\frac{2}{3}}LV^2]-yP}{P} 100\,\%$$

$$\frac{\dfrac{36{,}500V}{L+n_LV}[(f-t)C-xT-qklD^{\frac{2}{3}}LV^2]}{P} - 100yP\,\%$$

$$\frac{36{,}500V[(f-t)C-xT-qklD^{\frac{2}{3}}LV^2]}{(L+n_LV)P} - 100y\,\%$$

which is that quoted.

Dr Tutin, then expanded this to allow for the carriage of a weight of bunkers sufficient for the distance to be steamed, plus a margin for emergencies.[1] Writing:

C' for [load displacement – (light weight + stores)] and

r for a reserve factor for fuel (suggesting 4/3 as a working value)

he further added a factor ϕ for what he describes as 'the personal element...danger of the vessel not being continuously supplied with cargoes...and other contingencies'—i.e. risk and uncertainty. For purposes of comparison, however, he suggested it should be taken as unity; it is therefore omitted below.

Dr Tutin's revised formula is:

$$E = \frac{36{,}500V[(f-t)C'-xT-(q+rf-rt)klD^{\frac{2}{3}}LV^2]}{(L+n_LV)P} - 100y\,\%.$$

A simplified version of this formula with a somewhat different notation and without the allowance for a reserve of fuel was employed by G. S. Baker.[2]

APPENDIX 2

1. Introduction

This Appendix contains a worked example of the calculation of net present value on a hypothetical ship. The assumptions as to initial,

[1] *The economic efficiency of merchant ships*, art. cit.
[2] In *Ship efficiency and economy* (Birchall, 1942), and *Ship design resistance and screw propulsion* (Birchall, 1949).

capital and operating costs and revenues are purely for purposes of
exposition. Thus, the type of ship is irrelevant. (By current standards
the yield is quite high, at least for conventional types of ship.) It
should not be inferred that either the figures (except those of tax,
which are highly simplified) or the assumptions are necessarily
thought to be the best for current circumstances.

2. Assumptions

(*a*) Initial cost £1,260,000, of which £1,250,000 is capital for tax
purposes.
(*b*) Positive component of cash flow £520,000 p.a. in a full year's
operation.
(*c*) Operating costs £360,000 p.a. in a full year's operation.
(*d*) Tax and allowances at current United Kingdom rates.
(*e*) Survey periods and costs as in Table 4.1. A year of grace is
taken on each Special Survey (SS), but not cumulatively.

TABLE 4.1 *Survey periods and costs*

Year (1)	Survey (2)	Period (3)	Cost (4)
			£
5	No. 1 SS	Nil	10,000
9	No. 2 SS	Nil	20,000
13	No. 3 SS	36 days	40,000
17	2nd No. 1 SS	72 days	70,000
21	2nd No. 2 SS	108 days	100,000

Thus Nos. 1 and 2 Special Surveys are carried out without interrupting the ordinary trading of the ship.
(*f*) Life of vessel 25 complete years.
(*g*) Scrap value 5 % of capital cost = £62,500.
(*h*) Rate of discount 7 % in real terms and after tax.
(*i*) There are no general price changes during the life of the ship.
(*j*) There are no relative price changes during the life of the ship.
(*k*) There are no productivity changes during the life of the ship.
(*l*) The owners finance the ship from their own resources.
(*m*) The owners have profits from other sources sufficient to enable
them to take immediate advantage of the tax allowances.

3. Calculations

(a) Positive cash flow

This is simply the £520,000 p.a., specified in assumption (b), constant throughout (because it is being maintained in real terms), suitably adjusted by lay-up periods for surveys and by the scrap value.

TABLE 4.2 *The effect of surveys on positive cash flow*

Year (1)	Normal positive component of cash flow (£) (2)	Reduction for survey periods (£) (3)	Positive component of cash flow adjusted for surveys (£) (4) = (2)−(3)
1	520,000	Nil	520,000
2	520,000	Nil	520,000
3	520,000	Nil	520,000
4	520,000	Nil	520,000
5	520,000	Nil	520,000
6	520,000	Nil	520,000
7	520,000	Nil	520,000
8	520,000	Nil	520,000
9	520,000	Nil	520,000
10	520,000	Nil	520,000
11	520,000	Nil	520,000
12	520,000	Nil	520,000
13	520,000	51,300	468,700
14	520,000	Nil	520,000
15	520,000	Nil	520,000
16	520,000	Nil	520,000
17	520,000	102,600	417,400
18	520,000	Nil	520,000
19	520,000	Nil	520,000
20	520,000	Nil	520,000
21	520,000	153,900	366,100
22	520,000	Nil	520,000
23	520,000	Nil	520,000
24	520,000	Nil	520,000
25	582,500	Nil	582,500
26	Nil	Nil	Nil

(*b*) *Negative cash flow* (before tax)

This is simply the £360,000 p.a. specified in assumption (*c*) plus the survey costs.

TABLE 4.3 *The effect of surveys on negative cash flow*

Year (1)	Normal negative component of cash flow (2)	Survey costs (3)	Negative component of cash flow adjusted for surveys (4) = (2)+(3)
	£	£	£
1	360,000	Nil	360,000
2	360,000	Nil	360,000
3	360,000	Nil	360,000
4	360,000	Nil	360,000
5	360,000	10,000	370,000
6	360,000	Nil	360,000
7	360,000	Nil	360,000
8	360,000	Nil	360,000
9	360,000	20,000	380,000
10	360,000	Nil	360,000
11	360,000	Nil	360,000
12	360,000	Nil	360,000
13	360,000	40,000	400,000
14	360,000	Nil	360,000
15	360,000	Nil	360,000
16	360,000	Nil	360,000
17	360,000	70,000	430,000
18	360,000	Nil	360,000
19	360,000	Nil	360,000
20	360,000	Nil	360,000
21	360,000	100,000	460,000
22	360,000	Nil	360,000
23	360,000	Nil	360,000
24	360,000	Nil	360,000
25	360,000	Nil	360,000
26	Nil	Nil	Nil

(*c*) *Tax*

(N.B. The provisions cited in this example are highly simplified and will shortly become out of date.)

1. *Investment allowance:* This provides that taxable income shall be reduced by 40 % of the capital cost of the ship, effectively in the year following that in which the payment takes place.

Since the capital cost is £1,250,000 this reduction in taxable income is £500,000. With the tax rate at 53·75 % (= 7*s*. 9*d*. in the £ income tax plus 15 % profits tax) tax is reduced by £269,000 in year 1 of ship's life.

2. *Initial allowance:* The initial allowance on new ships was withdrawn in 1954.

3. *Depreciation allowance:* This provides that taxable income shall be reduced by a sum equal to 15 % of the book value for tax purposes in the previous year, again, effectively in the year following that in which the taxable income concerned is earned.

The effects of this are shown in Table 4.4.

TABLE 4.4 *The effect of depreciation allowance for tax*

Year (1)	Book value at end of year for tax purposes (2)	Depreciation allowance (3) = (2)×15 %	Reduction in tax at 53·75 % (4) = (3)×53.75 %	Effective reduction in tax (5)
	£	£	£	£
1	1,250,000	187,500	100,781	—
2	1,062,500	159,375	85,664	100,781
3	903,125	135,469	72,815	85,664
4	767,656	115,148	61,892	72,815
5	652,508	97,876	52,608	61,892
6	554,632	83,195	44,717	52,608
7	471,437	70,716	38,010	44,717
8	400,721	60,108	32,308	38,010
9	340,613	51,092	27,462	32,308
10	289,521	43,428	23,343	27,462
11	246,093	36,914	19,841	23,343
12	209,179	31,377	16,865	19,841
13	177,802	26,670	14,335	16,865
14	151,132	22,670	12,185	14,335
15	128,462	19,269	10,357	12,185
16	109,193	16,379	8,804	10,357
17	92,814	13,922	7,483	8,804
18	78,892	11,834	6,361	7,483
19	67,058	10,059	5,407	6,361
20	56,999	8,550	4,596	5,407
21	48,449	7,267	3,906	4,596
22	41,182	6,177	3,320	3,906
23	35,005	5,251	2,822	3,320
24	29,754	4,463	2,399	2,822
25	25,291	3,794	2,039	2,399
26	—	—	—	2,039

4. *Balancing charge:* This provides that if, when the ship is scrapped, the scrap value is greater than the written-down value for tax purposes, the difference becomes taxable. Thus the change in taxable income to allow for the balancing charge is 5 % of £1,250,000–£25,291.

5. *Tax payable:* Income Tax, at 7s. 9d. in the £ and Profits Tax at 15 % are payable with an average delay of one year.

This is shown in Table 4.5 as a total of 53·75 %.

TABLE 4.5 *Calculation of effective level of tax*

Year (1)	Before tax (£) Positive cash flow (2) (Table 4.2)	Negative cash flow (3) (Table 4.3)	Net cash flow (4) (2)−(3)	Tax allowances (£) (5) (See text and col. 3 of Table 4.4)	Taxable income (£) (6) (4)−(5)	Tax at 53·75 % (£) (7) (6)×53·75 %	Effective tax (£) (8) (7) delayed 1 year
1	520,000	360,000	160,000	687,500	−527,500	−283,531*	—
2	520,000	360,000	160,000	159,375	625	336	−283,531*
3	520,000	360,000	160,000	135,469	24,531	13,185	336
4	520,000	360,000	160,000	115,148	44,852	24,108	13,185
5	520,000	370,000	150,000	97,876	52,124	28,017	24,108
6	520,000	360,000	160,000	83,195	76,805	41,283	28,017
7	520,000	360,000	160,000	70,716	89,284	47,990	41,283
8	520,000	360,000	160,000	60,108	99,892	53,692	47,990
9	520,000	380,000	140,000	51,092	88,908	47,788	53,692
10	520,000	360,000	160,000	43,428	116,572	62,657	47,788
11	520,000	360,000	160,000	36,914	123,086	66,159	62,657
12	520,000	360,000	160,000	31,377	128,623	69,135	66,159
13	468,700	400,000	68,700	26,670	42,030	22,591	69,135
14	520,000	360,000	160,000	22,670	137,330	73,815	22,591
15	520,000	360,000	160,000	19,269	140,731	75,643	73,815
16	520,000	360,000	160,000	16,379	143,621	77,196	75,643
17	417,400	430,000	−12,600	13,922	−26,522	−14,256*	77,196
18	520,000	360,000	160,000	11,834	148,166	79,639	−14,256*
19	520,000	360,000	160,000	10,059	149,941	80,593	79,639
20	520,000	360,000	160,000	8,550	151,450	81,404	80,593
21	366,100	460,000	−93,900	7,267	−101,167	−54,377*	81,404
22	520,000	360,000	160,000	6,177	153,823	82,680	−54,377*
23	520,000	360,000	160,000	5,251	154,749	83,178	82,680
24	520,000	360,000	160,000	4,463	155,537	83,601	83,178
25	582,500	360,000	222,500	33,415†	255,915	137,554	83,601
26							137,554

* i.e. the tax on the whole of the rest of the enterprise will be reduced by this amount
† i.e. depreciation allowance (£3,794) minus the balancing charge of the excess of scrap value (£62,500) over written down value for tax purposes (£25,291).

(*d*) Calculation of negative cash flow after tax

TABLE 4.6

Year (1)	Negative cash flow before tax (£) (2)	Effective tax (£) (3)	Negative cash flow after tax (£) (4) = (2)+(3)
1	360,000	—	360,000
2	360,000	−283,531	76,469
3	360,000	336	360,336
4	360,000	13,185	373,185
5	370,000	24,108	394,108
6	360,000	28,017	388,017
7	360,000	41,283	401,283
8	360,000	47,990	407,990
9	380,000	53,692	433,692
10	360,000	47,788	407,788
11	360,000	62,657	422,657
12	360,000	66,159	426,159
13	400,000	69,135	469,135
14	360,000	22,591	382,591
15	360,000	73,815	433,815
16	360,000	75,463	435,643
17	430,000	77,196	507,196
18	360,000	−14,256	345,744
19	360,000	79,639	439,639
20	360,000	80,593	440,593
21	460,000	81,404	541,593
22	360,000	−54,377	305,623
23	360,000	82,680	442,680
24	360,000	83,178	443,178
25	360,000	83,601	443,601
26	Nil	137,554	137,554

(e) Calculation of net present value

(where opportunity cost of capital = 7 % after tax and in real terms)

TABLE 4.7

Year = i (1)	Cash flows after tax (£)			Discount factor = $(1+0.07)^{-i}$ (5)	Discounted cash flows (£) $A_i(1+0.07)^{-i}$ (6) = (4)×(5)
	Positive (2)	Negative (3)	Net = A_i (4) = (2)−(3)		
1	520,000	360,000	160,000	0·934579	149,533
2	520,000	76,469	443,531	0·873439	387,397
3	520,000	360,336	159,664	0·816298	130,333
4	520,000	373,185	146,815	0·762895	112,004
5	520,000	394,108	125,892	0·712986	89,759
6	520,000	388,017	131,983	0·666342	87,946
7	520,000	401,283	118,717	0·622750	73,931
8	520,000	407,990	112,010	0·582009	65,191
9	520,000	433,692	86,308	0·543934	46,946
10	520,000	407,788	112,212	0·508349	57,043
11	520,000	422,657	97,343	0·475093	46,247
12	520,000	426,159	93,841	0·444012	41,667
13	468,700	469,135	−435	0·414964	−181
14	520,000	382,591	137,409	0·387817	52,290
15	520,000	433,815	86,185	0·362446	31·237
16	520,000	435,643	84,357	0·338735	28,575
17	417,400	507,196	−89,796	0·316574	−28,427
18	520,000	345,744	174,256	0·295864	51,556
19	520,000	439,639	80,361	0·276508	22,220
20	520,000	440,593	79,407	0·258419	20,520
21	366,600	541,404	−175,404	0·241513	−42,362
22	520,000	305,623	214,377	0·225713	48,388
23	520,000	443,680	77,320	0·210947	16,310
24	520,000	443,178	76,822	0·197147	15,145
25	582,500	443,601	138,899	0·184249	25,592
26		137,554	−137,554	0·172195	−23,686

Total $\Sigma A_i(1+0.07)^{-i}$ = £1,506,174
Less initial cost = C = £1,260,000

NPV = $(\Sigma A_i(1+0.07)^{-i}) - C$ = £246,174

(*f*) *Calculation of yield*

(1) *Calculation of net present value* (*at* 10 %)

TABLE 4.8

Year = i (1)	Cash flows (£) Col. 4 of Table 4.7 Net = A_i (2)	Discount factor $(1+0\cdot10)-i$ (3)	Discounted cash flows (£) $A_i(1+0\cdot10)-i$ (4) = (2)×(3)
1	160,000	0·909091	145,455
2	443,531	0·826446	366,554
3	159,664	0·751315	119,957
4	146,815	0·683013	100,277
5	125,892	0·620921	78,169
6	131,983	0·564474	74,501
7	118,717	0·513158	60,921
8	112,010	0·466507	52,253
9	86,308	0·424098	36,603
10	112,212	0·385543	43,263
11	97,343	0·350494	34,118
12	93,841	0·318631	29,901
13	−435	0·289664	−126
14	137,409	0·263331	36,184
15	86,185	0·239392	20,632
16	84,357	0·217629	18,359
17	−89,796	0·197845	−17,766
18	174,256	0·179859	31,342
19	80,361	0·163508	13,140
20	79,407	0·148644	11,803
21	−175,404	0·135131	−23,703
22	214,377	0·122846	26,335
23	77,320	0·111678	8,635
24	76,822	0·101526	7,799
25	10,344	0·092296	955
26	(negative value removed by discounting to previous year at 7 % and subtracting from that year)*		

Total = $\Sigma A_i(1+0\cdot10)^{-i}$ = £1,275,601
Less initial cost = £1,260,000

NPV = $(\Sigma A_i(1+0\cdot10)^{-i})+C$ = £15,601

* This is not necessary in this instance but is included as an example of the 'extended yield' method.

7

GSI

(2) *Calculation of net present value (at 11 %)*

TABLE 4.9

Year = i (1)	Cash flows (£) Col. 4 of Table 4.7 Net = A_i (2)	Discount factor = $(1+0.11)^{-i}$ (3)	Discounted cash flows (£) $A_i(1+0.11)^{-i}$ (4) = (2)×(3)
1	160,000	0·900901	144,144
2	443,531	0·811622	359,980
3	159,664	0·731191	116,745
4	146,815	0·658731	96,712
5	125,892	0·593451	74,711
6	131,983	0·534641	70,564
7	118,717	0·481658	57,181
8	112,010	0·433926	48,604
9	86,308	0·390925	33,740
10	112,212	0·352184	39,519
11	97,343	0·317384	30,885
12	93,841	0·285841	26,824
13	−435	0·257514	−112
14	137,409	0·231995	31,878
15	86,185	0·209004	18,013
16	84,357	0·188292	15,884
17	−89,796	0·169633	−15,232
18	174,256	0·152822	26,630
19	80,361	0·137678	11,064
20	79,407	0·124034	9,849
21	−175,404	0·111742	−19,600
22	214,377	0·100669	21,581
23	77,320	0·090693	7,012
24	76,822	0·081705	6,277
25	10,344	0·073608	761
26			

Total = $\Sigma A_i(1+0.11)^{-i}$ = £1,213,614
Less initial cost = £1,260,000

NPV = $(\Sigma A_i(1+0.11)^{-i})-C$ = −£46,386

4. Results

At the cost of capital (7 % in real terms after tax) the net present value of this design with these assumptions is +£246,174. Unless an alternative can be found (e.g. another design, another method of financing or another date of commencement) with a greater net present value this project should be accepted.

The net present value at 10 % is +£15,601.

The net present value at 11 % is −£46,386.

The yield is therefore $10\dfrac{15{,}601}{61{,}987} = 10{\cdot}3\,\%.$

5

THE ECONOMICS OF AUTOMATION IN BRITISH SHIPPING

Introduction

Recent years have seen a marked acceleration of the rate at which shipowners have been installing equipment designed to improve the performance of their ships, to reduce costs and, in particular, to reduce the size of the crew that is carried. A considerable literature has grown up about the technical, operational and safety aspects of this, which, whether it involves feedback processes or not, is generally referred to in the shipping world as automation. The object of this paper is to provide some discussion of the economic (as distinct from technical or safety) factors which a shipowner might bear in mind when considering the installation of capital equipment intended to increase the profitability of a particular ship.

Such automation, which an economist would term increased capital-intensity, may provide benefits in many different ways: it may improve performance, as an automatic helmsman will if it steers a straighter course than a human one or as a data-logger may by increasing the accuracy and availability of data or by concentrating attention only upon the data relevant to any given problem; it may lengthen the time between maintenance or repair periods and, by a more precise indication of the condition of the equipment it is monitoring, enable breakdown to be prevented; it may hasten reaction to unusual or dangerous circumstances either by substituting its own reaction for a human one or by removing a human link from the chain of command as when engine controls can be operated direct from the bridge; or it may be intended simply to reduce the size of the ship's crew. Any given proposal for automation may include any or all of these and there is no valid economic generalization or formula which is applicable to all these circumstances, save one: that if the present value[1] of the net benefits exceeds the capital cost of the

---

[1] See above, pp. 61–99.

equipment then the ship will be more profitable with the item of equipment than without it. This, however, involves calculations typically occupying about one (trained) man-hour each and containing detailed estimates of present costs and future savings. A second object of this paper, therefore, is to discuss and present short-cut techniques which, with the aid of ready-reckoners, can reduce calculation time to an insignificant level. These ready-reckoners are intended for practical everyday use by all those to whom the assumptions seem reasonable. A third object is to reduce the need for precise estimation by altering the form of the information needed from:

'what are the costs, cost savings and revenue increases involved?'
    (which implies that we know all of these)
to:
'is the initial cost less than this?'
or:
'are the savings greater than this?'
    (which imply that we can estimate either the savings or the initial costs but not necessarily both).

A fourth object is to describe the effects of recent changes in United Kingdom fiscal arrangements so that the appropriate changes can be made in the example given in Appendix 2 to the earlier paper. A revised version is shown in Appendix 1 to this paper.

For convenience in following the equations the symbols employed are summarized, together with their definitions and assumed values, in a separate Table placed immediately before the ready-reckoners.

THE ECONOMIC EFFECTS OF AUTOMATION IN SHIPS

Where the object of some piece of capital equipment is to reduce the crew, and possibly in other instances, there may be a number of associated changes and these may occur in capital or operating costs, in revenues or in all three. Examples of savings in capital costs are:

crew accommodation,
crockery, cutlery and linen,
galley space and equipment,
life-saving equipment,
stores space.

To produce the true effect all such changes in ships' capital costs must be allowed for and the changes referred to later in this paper assume that this has been done, at least in broad terms. The changes in operating costs may include savings of:

wages,
overtime,
fringe benefits, including leave pay, repatriation and medical costs
food and food preparation
fuel for cooking, heating, cooling and electricity
fresh water
maintenance of accommodation and life-saving gear.

Some of these items will often be small or even zero. But some of the changes may be discrete; for example the saving of any one man in the deck department will probably have no effect on the number employed in the catering department; yet in any series of reductions in the deck crew there must come a time when the number of cooks and stewards can also be reduced. At such a point, therefore, the effect on operating and capital cost savings may be roughly doubled (if the first reduction is of a crew-member whose costs are about the same as those of the consequentially-saved member of the catering department). This, of course, is only one aspect of the fact that all these effects will appear in an incremental rather than in an average sense.

Again the saving of weight and space associated with the elimination of accommodation, etc., may cause an improvement in the earning capacity of the ship. This effect may often be fairly small and it will, of course, depend on their being cargo available to fill the increased capacity. Some forms of automation may also reduce repair costs and times, increase cargo-handling speeds or reduce the time of sea passages; any of these will lead to a greater number of voyages during the life of the ship and thus to enhanced revenue.

Although some of these associated effects may sometimes be small, there are many of them; it is, therefore, important to take into account, as far as possible, all the potential changes associated with the decision being considered. The rest of this paper assumes that all such effects have (at least in broad terms) been taken into account.

Methods

1. GENERAL

The methods (principally that of maximizing net present value) appropriate for the comparison of ship designs intended for similar purposes have been dealt with in an earlier paper and this paper brings the calculation methods up to date in terms of tax, etc., and offers various short-cut techniques. In brief, calculating the net present value entails discounting the net benefits by multiplying them, year by year, by discount factors and summing the products. The discount factor is $(1+r)^{-i}$,

where

r represents the rate of discount (e.g. $0.06 = 6\%$) per year
and

i represents the interval in years between fitting the equipment and obtaining the benefit.

Discount factors for any reasonable range of values of r and i may be obtained from financial tables. The general formula for this purpose is:

$$\text{Net present value (NPV)} = \sum_{i=0}^{i=n} (R_i - C_i)(1+r)^{-i}, \qquad (1)$$

where

n is the economic life of the equipment concerned,

R_i is the change in gross earnings in year i (resulting from the automation proposal) and

C_i is the change in gross costs in year i (resulting from the automation proposal), including, for year 0 (when R_i is probably zero), the capital costs. Any taxes (net of allowances) that may be payable and investment grants receivable should also be included as and when they occur.

Where the capital cost is to be paid off in the year of construction this formula may be written:

$$\text{NPV} = \sum_{i=1}^{i=n} (R_i - C_i)(1+r)^{-i} - C_0 \qquad (2)$$

and this has the advantage of treating the initial cost separately. Where there is a choice between one piece of equipment and another, and except where different ship life expectancies are involved, the one that gives the greatest value of NPV is economically the best. $(R_i - C_i)$ is often written as A_i and defined as net cash flow—hence this technique is often called discounted cash flow or d.c.f. Alternatively, $(R_i - C_i)$ may be expanded into $(P_i Q_i - C_i)$ where P represents the freight rate and Q the quantity of cargo concerned.

2. TAXATION

As noted above, it is necessary to take account of the tax system relevant to the shipowner concerned. The tax system applicable to shipowners resident in the United Kingdom (some of whom may also have tax liabilities in other countries) has recently undergone fundamental changes. In brief, the former system involved income tax and profits tax (with the former at 7s. 9d. in the £ and the latter at 15 % the total was 53·75 %; with income tax as 8s. 3d. in the £ and profits tax at 15 % the total was 56·25 %) on taxable income. Before taxable income for any one year was arrived at, certain allowances were deductible; the principal ones were an investment allowance of 40 % of the capital costs of ships paid in the year in question and a depreciation allowance of 15 % of the capital cost on the reducing balance system. There was also provision for a balancing charge if the resale price of the ship (either during its life or at scrapping) exceeded the written-down value of the ship at the date concerned. In other words, if the resale price exceeded the historic capital cost minus the total depreciation allowed for tax purposes to that date, the difference became taxable. Taxes were collected with an average lag of between one and two years.

The new system differs from the previous one in two principal ways: first, the tax allowances are changed in that the 40 % investment allowance is abolished and replaced by a 20 %[1] cash grant[2] and in that depreciation may be taken at any rate the shipowner chooses,[3] and secondly in that the tax liability depends not only on the taxable income but also on how much of it is distributed to the shareholders. (The following description is necessarily somewhat simplified and omits the transitional provisions due to expire in 1975.)

[1] Between 1 Jan. 1967 and 31 Dec. 1968 this is increased to 25 %. See Appendix 2.
[2] Investment incentives, Comnd. 2874. HMSO, January 1966.
[3] Finance Act, 1965, Part II, sec. 14, subsect. (1).

The cash grant is a simple 20 % of the capital cost of the ship, including its equipment. It is payable by the Board of Trade with a lag of about 1 year and it is hoped, ultimately, to reduce this lag to about six months. Thus, while the investment allowance was of value only to those shipowners with sufficient profits to take advantage of it, the investment grant is of equal value to all. Because of the cash grant, depreciation is now allowed only on the remaining 80 % of the ship's capital cost; but it can be taken freely, i.e. at any rate that the shipowner wishes. It is obviously to his advantage to take the allowance as soon as possible, since he thereby postpones tax payments—but whether he can do so depends on whether he has sufficient profits (presumably from other sources; who could expect a ship to earn a gross profit of 80 % of its capital cost in one year?) against which to set it.

The second major change is the introduction of differentiation in the tax liability of a company according to the proportion of profits distributed to the shareholders. The taxable income (i.e. gross profits minus allowances) is taxed at a corporation tax rate announced in the Chancellor's annual Budget Speech (the current rate is 40 %) and, in addition, that part which is distributed as dividends is taxed at the income tax rate applicable to the individual recipients—in most instances the standard rate. Regardless of whether there was any corporation tax liability for the year in question this income tax must actually be paid to the Inland Revenue. A firm which ploughs back a large proportion of its profits will therefore pay less tax than before and one which distributes a large proportion to its shareholders will pay more. The lag in the collection of taxes seems likely to remain unchanged. The total of corporation and income taxes cannot, therefore, be assessed without knowing the company's policy of dividend distribution. Moreover, since one of the objects of the new tax system is to encourage the ploughing-back of profits into productive investment, it is obvious that the distribution policies of the past are not necessarily any guide to the future. The best way to allow for tax in considering the automation of ships is, therefore, to ignore income tax altogether and assume only a rate of corporation tax.

However, just as the old investment allowances were of the greatest value to shipowners with sufficient profits to take immediate advantage of them (and in recent years these have been very few), so the same is true of the free depreciation allowance. Under both the new and the old tax systems, therefore, it is impossible to calculate the present value of taxation without assuming some level of taxable profits from assets other than the ship in question. In present circumstances there are some shipowners who seem likely to have no tax liability whatever (except, of course, for accounting to the Inland Revenue for the income tax deducted from dividends) for some considerable time to come. Many shipowners will find themselves somewhere between this extreme position and the opposite, but equally extreme, position of having sufficient profits to take full and immediate advantage of the free depreciation allowance. It may, however,be noted that it is possible to have a tax position outside this range; for if the shipowner concerned has little in the form of unused tax allowances and his gross profits are large the free depreciation allowances will soon be fully absorbed and corporation tax will be payable on his gross profits thereafter. How soon this occurs will, of course, depend on the size of his unused tax allowances, if any, and the investment pattern and profitability of the whole of his enterprise; but it seems probable that the unused investment allowances would have to be very small, and the profitability quite large before the liability for corporation tax became sufficiently large, and came sufficiently early in the ship's life, to make a great deal of difference to the calculations shown in the rest of this paper. Precision in the type of calculations described here can, therefore, be achieved only by the shipowner concerned; but it is useful to consider the first two tax positions mentioned above for they define the area within which the typical British shipowner is likely to find himself.

As noted above, however, their position will be the same in one respect: they will all receive the 20 % cash grant. Since this will (at least initially) be paid with an average lag of about $1\frac{1}{2}$ years, some discounting is necessary to express this in terms of present value, partly to allow for the deferring of the receipt and partly to allow for any possible change in the value of money during this lag. Table 5.1 shows the present value equivalents of 20 % investment grants at a variety of discount rates and lags and is simply the solution of:

$$G_{PV} = G_N(1+r_m)^{-l}, \tag{3}$$

TABLE 5.1. *Present value of investment grant,* $G_{PV} = G_N(1+r_m)^{-l}$

Rate of discount r_m (%)	Lag in receipt of grant (years, %)		
	1	1·5	2
5	19·048	18·589	18·141
6	18·868	18·326	17·800
7	18·692	18·070	17·469
8	18·519	17·819	17·147
9	18·348	17·575	16·834
10	18·182	17·336	16·529

TABLE 5.2. **Factor B**. *Capital cost after allowing for present value of investment grant,* $B = (1-G_{PV}) = 1-G_N(1+r_m)^{-l}$

Rate of discount r_m (%)	Lag in receipt of grant, l (years)		
	1	1·5	2
5	0·80952	0·81411	0·81859
6	0·81132	0·81674	0·82200
7	0·81308	0·81930	0·82531
8	0·81481	0·82181	0·82853
9	0·81652	0·82425	0·83166
10	0·81818	0·82664	0·83471

where G_{PV} is the present value equivalent of the nominal rate G_N, l is the lag in receipt (measured in years) and r_m is the discount rate in money terms (i.e. including any expected rate of inflation). If we write r_r for the rate of discount in real terms and r_p for the rate of change in prices in general then:

$$r_m = (1+r_r)(1+r_p)-1$$

thus, if $r_r = 6\%$ p.a. and $r_p = 3\%$ p.a., $r_m = 9·18\%$ p.a. The smaller are r_r and r_p the nearer does r_m come to (r_r+r_p).

For some purposes, however, the value that is wanted is not the present value of the investment grant but the present value of the capital cost after allowing for the grant. Obviously, this is simply $(1-G_{PV})$. Values are shown in Table 5.2.

3. THE NO-TAX POSITION

Although the investment allowance is no longer given unused allowances can still be carried forward from previous years. If the shipowner concerned has accumulated tax allowances from earlier years so great that he is unlikely, given the prospective level of his aggregate profits, to have any taxable income for the indefinite future, then, regardless of the profits expected from the given proposal, the free depreciation allowance is of no value to him. This, as well as the rate of corporation tax, may then be ignored.

(a) A constant improvement in net cash flow

If the proposed equipment is estimated to lead to an improvement in net cash flow of £A, which will subsequently be maintained at a constant level in real terms, then (neglecting the investment grant for the time being) the discounting can be done in one step by solving:

$$\text{NPV} = A \left\{ \frac{1-(1+r_r)^{-n}}{r_r} \right\} - C_0. \tag{4}$$

Values of $\dfrac{1-(1+r)^{-n}}{r}$ may be obtained, for any reasonable values of r

and n, from annuity tables. If $r = 6\%$ and $n = 20$ the value is 11·4699. If both A and C_0 are known the calculation is simple and speedy. But if, as is very likely, one or the other is extremely difficult to estimate we must approach the problem differently.

If we seek the *minimum* improvement in net cash flow necessary to justify a given addition to the ship's capital cost (and allowing for the cash grant), and if this improvement may reasonably be expected to remain constant in real terms over the ship's life, it is defined by:

$$\text{NPV} = \text{zero} = A \left\{ \frac{1-(1+r_r)^{-n}}{r_r} \right\} - C_0 B, \tag{5}$$

whence

$$A_{\text{min.}} = \frac{C_0 B}{\left\{ \dfrac{1-(1+r_r)^{-n}}{r_r} \right\}}. \tag{6}$$

(Here, as elsewhere in this paper, the 'justification' might or might not be regarded as sufficient by a shipowner. Strictly, this value of A

is that level which will make the shipowner indifferent as to whether the proposal is adopted or not.)

If we assume $r = 0.06$ throughout (i.e. that $r_r = r_m$),

$$G_N = 0.2, \quad n = 20 \text{ years} \quad \text{and} \quad l = 1.5 \text{ years}$$

then $A_{\min} = 0.0712C_0$ and $C_{0\max} = 14.04353A$.

Thus, a net increase of £10,000 in the capital cost of a ship requires, on these assumptions, an improvement in net cash flow of *at least* £712 p.a. to justify it and, similarly, it is worth spending *up to* £14,044 more on the capital cost of a ship in order to obtain a net cash flow improvement of £1,000 p.a., constant in real terms.

The equality of r_r and r_m assumed here implies a zero rate of inflation and this may not be in accordance with the shipowner's expectations. If we assume an inflation-rate of 3 % p.a., r_m will be approximately 9 % and, retaining the other assumptions,

$$A_{\min} = 0.07186C_0 \quad \text{and} \quad C_{0\max} = 13.9155A.$$

It is immediately obvious that these figures are very close to those obtained when zero inflation is assumed or, in other words, that inflation (at rates in the region of 3 % p.a.) is not very important in this context.

Ready-reckoner 1 A at the end of this paper shows, as the left-hand figure on each line, the maximum net increase in capital cost that it is worth paying in order to obtain the constant improvement in net cash flow shown in the stub. Ready-reckoner 2 A shows, again as the left-hand figure on each line, the minimum net cash flow improvement necessary, on these assumptions, to justify the net increase in capital cost shown in the stub. Zero inflation and a no-tax position are assumed. Investment grants are taken into account.

(b) A geometrically continuing improvement in net cash flow

So far we have dealt only with an improvement in net cash flow which is constant in real terms. Obviously this may be the case: but if the advantages of a given proposal come largely from reducing the size of the crew then it may be more reasonable to assume that, because seamens' earnings are likely, in real terms, to keep pace with the growth of per capita real income in the economy as a whole, the

saving starts at some given level and increases geometrically thereafter. This may be a more realistic assumption than the former even
when the proposal is likely to be accompanied by repair costs
(associated with the automation proposal being considered) which
also rise geometrically; for if the repair costs are initially less than the
saving in crew costs, etc., and increase geometrically at any rate less
than the rate of increase of crew costs then there must be a geometrically increasing gap between them. It is this gap which is the
improvement in net cash flow.

If we write this rate of growth in net cash flow as g and take the
likeliest assumption of $g < r$, then the present value of a series of net
cash flows starting at A_1, growing at $g \%$ p.a. and extending for
n years is:

$$C = A_1 \left[\frac{1 - \left(\frac{1+g}{1+r}\right)^n}{r-g} \right]. \tag{7}$$

If we maintain the assumptions given earlier and further assume that
$g = 3 \%$ p.a. (i.e. that $g = 0.03$) then:

$$C = 14.56150 A_1.$$

Table 5.3 shows values of C for various combinations of r and g.

If we seek the minimum initial improvement in net cash flow
necessary to justify a given net addition to the ship's capital cost
then, on this basis, it is defined by:

$$\text{NPV} = \text{zero} = 14.56150 A_1 - C_0 B, \tag{8}$$

whence $A_{1\min} = 0.05609 C_0$ and $C_{0\max} = 17.82883 A_1$.

Thus, a net increase of £10,000 in a ship's capital cost leading to an
improvement in net cash flow increasing in real terms at 3% p.a. for
20 years requires the initial improvement in net cash flow to be *at
least* £561 to justify it; and similarly, it is worth while spending *up to*
£17,829 more on the capital cost of a ship in order to obtain an initial
improvement in net cash flow of £1,000, increasing thereafter at 3%
p.a. in real terms for 20 years.

Ready-reckoner 1 B at the end of this paper shows, as the left-hand
figure on each line, the maximum net increase in capital cost that is
worth paying, on these assumptions, in order to obtain the initial

TABLE 5.3. **Factor C.** *Present values, at various rates of discount, of 20-year net cash flows increasing geometrically at various rates of growth*

Rate of discount (r) per year (%)	Rate of growth (g) per year (%)						
	2	3	4	5	6	7	8
5	14·6654	15·9644	17·4168	19·0476	20·8738	22·9222	25·1824
6	13·4169	14·5615	15·8379	17·2692	18·8679	20·6591	22·6640
7	12·3201	13·3317	14·4047	15·7173	17·1211	18·6916	20·4481
8	11·3533	12·2501	13·2480	14·3579	15·5958	16·9773	18·5185
9	10·4980	11·2956	12·1811	13·1643	14·2584	15·4770	16·8337

improvement in net cash flow shown in the stub. Ready-reckoner 2 B shows, again as the left-hand figure on each line, the minimum initial net cash flow improvement necessary, on these assumptions, to justify the increase in capital cost shown in the stub. Zero inflation and a no-tax position are assumed. Investment grants are taken into account.

4. THE FULL-TAX POSITION

(a) *The calculation of tax and tax allowances*

Where the shipowner has sufficient profits (from sources other than the proposal in question) to enable him to take full advantage of the free depreciation allowance on the capital cost involved in the proposal itself then the net cash flow will be increased, about 1·5 years after the ship is built, by a reduction in the corporation tax which would otherwise have been payable. In other years corporation tax will be payable as if the depreciation allowance had not existed (since it will all have been used up). The investment grant will be unaffected. The following discussion takes these points into account but omits the rather unimportant (in terms of present value) balancing charge.

Because the investment grant covers 20 % of the capital cost, depreciation can only be allowed for the remaining 80 %. The depreciation allowance is thus $0·8C_0$, the reduction in the corporation

TABLE 5.4. **Factor D**. *Present value of free depreciation allowance*
$$D = (1 - G_N)tC_0(1 + r_m)^{-l}$$

Corporation tax t (%)	Rate of discount, r_m (%)				
	6	7	8	9	10
35	0·25657	0·25298	0·24947	0·24605	0·24270
36	0·26390	0·26020	0·25660	0·25308	0·24963
37	0·27123	0·26743	0·26373	0·26011	0·25657
37½	0·27489	0·27105	0·26729	0·26362	0·26004
38	0·27856	0·27466	0·27086	0·26714	0·26350
39	0·28589	0·28189	0·27798	0·27417	0·27044
40	0·29322	0·28912	0·28511	0·28120	0·27737
41	0·30055	0·29634	0·29224	0·28823	0·28431
42	0·30788	0·30357	0·29937	0·29526	0·29124
42½	0·31154	0·30719	0·30293	0·29877	0·29471
43	0·31521	0·31080	0·30650	0·30229	0·29817
44	0·32254	0·31803	0·31362	0·30932	0·30511
45	0·32987	0·32526	0·32075	0·31635	0·31204

tax payable is $0·8tC_0$ (where t is the rate of corporation tax) and the present value of the reduction in corporation tax is:

$$0·8tC_0(1 + r_m)^{-l}. \tag{9}$$

Because of the low value of the lag in the collection of taxes, expectations, if any, of inflation are unimportant in this context too. Table 5.4 shows the present value of the reduction in corporation tax due to taking free depreciation, in full, 1·5 years after the ship is built.

It remains to calculate the effects of corporation tax itself. This may most conveniently be done by calculating a factor by which the net cash flow for any given year must be multiplied in order to produce a net of tax figure for inclusion in a present value calculation. Writing E for such a factor we have:

$$E = 1 - t(1 + r_m)^{-l} \tag{10}$$

and, if we maintain our earlier assumptions:

$$E = 1 - 0·91631t$$

Table 5.5 shows values of E for various levels of corporation tax.

TABLE 5.5. **Factor E.** *Net of corporation tax Factor*

$$E = 1 - t(1+r_m)^{-l}, \text{ where } l = 1.5 \text{ years}$$

corporation tax t (%)	Rate of discount, r_m (%)				
	6	7	8	9	10
35	0·67929	0·68378	0·68816	0·69244	0·69663
36	0·67013	0·67474	0·67925	0·68365	0·68796
37	0·66097	0·66571	0·67034	0·67487	0·67929
37½	0·65639	0·66119	0·66589	0·67047	0·67496
38	0·65180	0·65667	0·66143	0·66608	0·67062
39	0·64264	0·64764	0·65252	0·65729	0·66195
40	0·63348	0·63860	0·64361	0·64850	0·65329
41	0·62431	0·62957	0·63470	0·63976	0·64462
42	0·61515	0·62053	0·62579	0·63093	0·63595
42½	0·61057	0·61602	0·62134	0·62653	0·63162
43	0·60599	0·61150	0·61688	0·62214	0·62728
44	0·59683	0·60246	0·60797	0·61335	0·61862
45	0·58766	0·59343	0·59906	0·60457	0·60995

(b) A constant improvement in net cash flow

Armed with these preliminary calculations we may now re-examine the calculations made in section 3 (*a*) above but this time from the point of view of a shipowner in the full-tax position just defined. Formula (5) may be expanded so as to allow, not only for the constant improvement in net cash flow, the rate of discount, the cash grant and the lag in its receipt but also for the maximum effects of free depreciation and corporation tax. The result is:

$$\text{NPV} = \text{zero} = AE\left\{\frac{1-(1+r_r)^{-n}}{r_r}\right\} - C_0 B + C_0 D, \qquad (11)$$

whence

$$A_{\min} = \frac{C_0 B - C_0 D}{E\left\{\dfrac{1-(1+r_r)^{-n}}{r_r}\right\}} \qquad (12)$$

of which the various components may easily be found. Factor B, the adjustment to the capital cost to allow for the investment grant and the lag in its receipt, has been calculated in Table 5.2; Factor D, the present value of the free depreciation allowance, has been calculated

8

in Table 5.4; Factor E, the adjustment for corporation tax and the lag in its payment has been calculated in Table 5.5; and

$$\left\{\frac{1-(1+r_r)^{-n}}{r_r}\right\},$$

the factor for reducing a constant flow of real values to its present value may, as noted earlier, be obtained from suitable annuity tables.

The only additional quantitative assumption needed for the solution of formula (12) is the rate of corporation tax and this may be taken at its current level of 40 %. We thus have:

$$A_{\min} = 0.07205C_0 \quad \text{and} \quad C_{0\max} = 13.87895A.$$

Thus, net increase of £10,000 in the capital cost of a ship requires, on these assumptions, an improvement in net cash flow of *at least* £721 to justify it. Similarly, it is worth while spending *up to* £13,879 more on a ship in order to obtain a net cash flow improvement of £1,000 p.a. constant and in real terms. It will be observed that these figures are very similar to those given in section 3 (*a*) above, which referred to a similar constant improvement in net cash flow when the effects of free depreciation and corporation tax might be ignored. This similarity means that less attention needs to be paid to the shipowner's tax position than might have been expected under the former tax system.

If we had (quite illegitimately) ignored the investment grant in section 3 (*a*) then we would have had simply:

$$A_{\min} = \frac{C_0}{11.4699} = 0.08718C_0 \quad \text{and} \quad C_{0\max} = 11.4699A.$$

These results which might, naively, be regarded as some sort of half-way house between the two extremes of having sufficient tax allowances to have no tax liability for the indefinite future and being able to take full advantage of the free depreciation allowance are in fact nothing of the kind. That the investment grant must *always* be taken into account is the only possible conclusion. However, if this is done, the similarity between the full-tax and no-tax positions remains.

Ready-reckoner 1A at the end of this paper shows, as the right-hand figure on each line, the maximum increase in capital cost that is worth paying in order to obtain the constant improvement in net cash flow shown in the stub. Zero inflation and a full-tax position are assumed. Ready-reckoner 2 A shows, again as the right-hand figure on each line, the minimum net cash flow improvement necessary, on these assumptions, to justify the net increase in capital cost shown in the stub.

(c) A geometrically continuing improvement in net cash flow

We may now re-examine the calculations made in section 3 (*b*) above but this time from the point of view of a shipowner in the full-tax position. Formula (8) may be expanded into:

$$\text{NPV} = \text{zero} = AEC - C_0 B + C_0 D \tag{13}$$

and again the principal components of this have already been calculated. On our earlier quantitative assumptions we obtain:

$$A_{1\min} = 0.05675 C_0 \quad \text{and} \quad C_{0\max} = 17.61989 A_1.$$

Thus a net increase of £10,000 in the capital cost of a ship requires, on these assumptions, an initial improvement in net cash flow of *at least* £568 to justify it. Similarly, it is worth while spending *up to* £17,620 more on a ship in order to obtain an initial net cash flow improvement of £1,000 increasing thereafter at 3 % p.a. for 20 years.

Ready-reckoner 1 B at the end of this paper shows, as the right-hand figure on each line, the maximum net increase in capital cost that it is worth paying, on these assumptions, in order to obtain the initial improvement in net cash flow shown in the stub. Ready-reckoner 2 B shows, again as the right-hand figure on each line, the minimum initial net cash flow improvement necessary, on these assumptions, to justify the increase in capital cost shown in the stub. Investment grants, depreciation allowances and corporation tax are all taken into account—i.e. a full-tax position is assumed. Zero inflation is again assumed.

5. THE EFFECTS OF INFLATION

The foregoing sections have implicitly assumed that, because inflation (at moderate rates) could be demonstrated to have only insignificant effects on the individual components of our equations, the effects of inflation on the final results must also be insignificant. It will, however, not have escaped notice that these components appear in com-

TABLE 5.6. *Comparison of results with and without 3 % p.a.*
inflation being assumed

	Zero inflation (£)	3 % inflation p.a. (£)	Difference (%)
Constant improvement in net cash flow			
No-tax position:			
Min. net cash flow improvement to justify £10,000 capital	712	718	+0·8
Max. capital cost increase for £1,000 in net cash flow	14,044	13,916	−0·9
Full-tax position:			
Min. net cash flow improvement to justify £10,000 capital	721	730	+1·2
Max. capital cost increase for £1,000 in net cash flow	13,879	13,697	−1·3
Geometric improvement in net cash flow			
No-tax position:			
Min. initial net cash flow improvement to justify £10,000 capital	561	566	+0·9
Max. capital cost increase for £1,000 in initial net cash flow	17,829	17,666	−0·9
Full-tax position:			
Min. initial net cash flow improvement to justify £10,000 capital	568	575	+1·2
Max. capital cost increase for £1,000 in initial net cash flow	17,620	17,389	−1·3

bination. It being undoubtedly true that many a mickle may make a muckle, we may now test the sensitivity of our results to a positive value for r_p; i.e. to an assumption that $r_m > r_r$ and by some significant amount. It may, however, be noted that this does not itself necessarily effect the value of r_r; for we should always be interested in the profitability of a project in real (constant purchasing power) terms, not in terms of any varying unit.

This test may conveniently be performed by assuming a 3 % p.a. rate of inflation and ignoring the point noted earlier that, strictly speaking, 1·03 times 1·06 is not 1·09 but 1·0918. Bearing in mind the margins of error in both assumptions 1·09 is near enough and may, therefore, be substituted for r_m in the appropriate places. Table 5.6 summarizes the earlier results and provides a comparison of these with the alternative assumption just suggested.

It will be seen from the right-hand column of this table that the differences are all negligible. The greatest is 1·3 % and the mean deviation (i.e. ignoring the signs) is 1·1 %. At rates in the region of 3 % (which is not far off the historical average for the United Kingdom since the war), therefore, inflation may be ignored without significant error in calculations of the type described.

Conclusions

This paper has described, in some detail, methods which may be applied to the solution of simple problems in the economics of ship automation. It has not dealt with the mutually exclusive case (i.e. shall we have this device or that one?) with the problem of timing (i.e. shall we have this device now or later?), nor has it dealt with cases where the improvement in net cash flow is neither constant nor geo-metrically increasing. For these, as for many other circumstances, detailed calculations will always be necessary. Moreover, it has assumed, in the text and in the ready-reckoners, values of the various equation components which some readers may find unacceptable. But the methods have been shown and the components of the final equations have been calculated for a variety of assumptions; it is therefore a simple matter for anyone who wishes to do so to produce ready-reckoners based on different quantitative assumptions. The reader may also produce ready-reckoners based on, for example, an arithmetically increasing net cash flow or a geometrically declining net cash flow.

Summary of symbols, definitions and values ascribed

Symbol	Definition	Value
A	Net cash flow per year (or change in net cash flow) due to capital expenditure	
A_i	Net cash flow in year i	
A_1	Net cash flow (or change in net cash flow due to capital expenditure) in the first year of ship's trading	

Symbol	Definition	Value
B	Factor for adjusting capital cost for the present value of the investment grant	0·81674
C	Present value of a geometrically increasing series of net cash flow	14·5614999
C_c	Capital cost when payable at start of ship's life	
C_i	Cash costs in year i	
C_0	Capital cost or change in capital cost due to an automation proposal	
D	Factor for adjusting capital cost for the present value of the free depreciation allowance	0·2932176
E	Net of corporation tax factor. Net cash flows, when multiplied by this factor are turned into their post-tax equivalents allowing for the lag in tax collections	0·63347800
g	Rate of growth of net cash flows	0·03 p.a.
G_N	Investment grant	20 %
G_{PV}	Present value equivalent of investment grant, i.e. allowing for lag in payment	18·326 %
i	A year of ship's life or in the life of the equipment concerned	
l	Lag (a) in receipt of investment grant; and (b) in payment of corporation tax	1·5 years
n	Ship's (economic) life, or life of proposed automation equipment	20 years
P_i	Freight rate in year i of ship's life	
Q_i	Quantity of cargo carried in year i of ship's life	
R_i	Revenue in year i	
r	A rate of discount	0·06
r_r	A rate of discount in real terms (the opportunity cost of capital)	0·06
r_m	A rate of discount in money terms	0·918
r_p	A rate of change in prices	0·03
t	A rate of corporation tax	0·40

Ready-reckoner 1A: Solution of net capital cost change equivalent to known constant net cash flow change. Left-hand figure no-tax, right-hand figure full tax basis.

Ready-reckoner 2B: Solution of net capital cost change equivalent to known initial level of geometrically increasing net cash flow change. Left-hand figure no-tax, right-hand figure full-tax basis.

Net cash flow change (£)	1A. Constant (tax position, £)		1B. Geometric growth (tax position, £)	
	No-tax	Full-tax	No-tax	Full-tax
100	1,404	1,388	1,783	1,762
200	2,809	2,776	3,566	3,524
300	4,213	4,164	5,349	5,286
400	5,617	5,552	7,132	7,048
500	7,022	6,939	8,914	8,810
600	8,426	8,327	10,697	10,572
700	9,830	9,715	12,480	12,334
800	11,235	11,103	14,263	14,096
900	12,639	12,491	16,046	15,858
1,000	14,044	13,879	17,829	17,620
1,500	21,065	20,818	26,743	26,430
2,000	28,087	27,758	35,658	35,240
2,500	35,109	34,697	44,572	44,050
3,000	42,131	41,637	53,486	52,860
3,500	49,152	48,576	62,401	61,670
4,000	56,174	55,516	71,315	70,480
4,500	63,196	62,455	80,230	79,290
5,000	70,218	69,395	89,144	88,099
6,000	84,261	83,274	106,973	105,719
7,000	98,305	97,153	124,802	123,339
8,000	112,348	111,032	142,631	140,959
9,000	126,392	124,911	160,459	158,579
10,000	140,435	138,790	178,288	176,199
15,000	210,653	208,184	267,432	264,298
20,000	280,871	277,579	356,577	352,398
30,000	421,306	416,369	534,865	528,597
40,000	561,741	555,158	713,153	704,796
50,000	702,177	693,948	891,441	880,995
60,000	842,612	832,737	1,069,730	1,057,193
70,000	983,047	971,527	1,248,018	1,233,392
80,000	1,123,482	1,110,316	1,426,306	1,409,591
90,000	1,263,918	1,249,106	1,604,595	1,585,790
100,000	1,404,353	1,387,795	1,782,883	1,761,989

N.B. Linear interpolation may be made vertically: not horizontally.

Ready-reckoner 2A: Solution of constant net cash flow change equivalent to known net capital cost change. Left-hand figure no-tax, right-hand figure full-tax basis.

Ready-reckoner 2B: Solution of net cash flow change equivalent to known initial level of geometrically increasing net cash flow change. Left-hand figure no-tax, right-hand figure full-tax basis.

Net capital cost change (£)	2A. Constant (tax position, £)		2B. Geometric growth (tax position, £)	
	No-tax	Full-tax	No-tax	Full-tax
100	7	7	6	6
200	14	14	11	11
300	21	22	17	17
400	28	29	22	23
500	36	36	28	28
600	43	43	34	34
700	50	50	39	40
800	57	58	45	45
900	64	65	50	51
1,000	71	72	56	57
1,500	107	108	84	85
2,000	142	144	112	114
2,500	178	180	140	142
3,000	214	216	168	170
3,500	249	252	196	199
4,000	285	288	224	227
4,500	320	324	252	255
5,000	356	360	280	284
6,000	427	432	337	341
7,000	498	504	393	397
8,000	570	576	449	454
9,000	641	648	505	511
10,000	712	721	561	568
15,000	1,068	1,081	841	851
20,000	1,424	1,441	1,122	1,135
30,000	2,136	2,162	1,683	1,703
40,000	2,848	2,882	2,244	2,270
50,000	3,560	3,603	2,804	2,838
60,000	4,272	4,323	3,365	3,405
70,000	4,985	5,044	3,926	3,973
80,000	5,697	5,764	4,487	4,540
90,000	6,409	6,485	5,048	5,108
100,000	7,121	7,205	5,609	5,675

N.B. Linear interpolation may be made vertically: not horizontally.

Acknowledgements

I am indebted to Messrs H. T. Beazley and A. W. Bowen (New Zealand Shipping Co. Ltd), J. Glyde (Shaw Savill and Albion Co. Ltd), N. G. A. Johnson (British & Commonwealth (Group Management) Ltd) and J. Mitchell (P. & O.) and to colleagues in HM Treasury and the Board of Trade for helpful comments on earlier drafts of this paper. I am indebted to HM Treasury and the Board of Trade for permission to publish it. I alone am responsible for the views expressed and for any errors and omissions.

APPENDIX 1

INTRODUCTION

This Appendix contains a worked example of the calculation of net present value on a hypothetical ship. A net present value calculation on any part of a ship would be carried out in exactly the same way. The example is very similar to that given in the earlier paper: indeed the only differences are in investment grants, the treatment of depreciation for tax purposes, the tax rate and the assumed lag in the collection of taxes, which has been increased from one year in the earlier example to a more realistic $1\frac{1}{2}$ years. Because of this, and because income tax has been ignored, the NPV is not directly comparable with that given in the earlier paper; it cannot be inferred from a comparison of the two examples that the new tax-plus-grant system is more favourable to British shipowners than the old system of taxes and tax allowances.

The assumptions as to initial capital and operating costs are purely for purposes of exposition. It should not be inferred that either the figures or the assumptions are necessarily thought to be the best for current circumstances. Extensive use is made of the short-cut methods employed in the body of the paper, and of the tables shown earlier.

ASSUMPTIONS

(*a*) Initial cost £1,260,000 of which £1,250,000 is capital for tax and investment grant purposes.
(*b*) Positive component of cash flow £520,000 p.a. in a full year's operation.
(*c*) Operating costs £360,000 p.a. in a full year's operation.
(*d*) Investment grant, tax and allowances at current United Kingdom rates.
(*e*) Survey periods and costs as in Table 5.A1. A year of grace is taken on each Special Survey, but not cumulatively.

TABLE 5.A1. *Survey periods and costs*

Year (1)	Survey (2)	Period (3)	Cost (4)
5	No. 1 SS	Nil	10,000
9	No. 2 SS	Nil	20,000
13	No. 3 SS	36 days	40,000
17	2nd No. 1 SS	72 days	70,000
21	2nd No. 2 SS	108 days	100,000

Thus Nos. 1 and 2 Special Surveys are carried out without interrupting the ordinary trading of the ship.

(*f*) Life of vessel 25 complete years.
(*g*) Scrap value 5 % of capital cost = £62,500.
(*h*) Rate of discount 7 % in real terms and after tax.
(*i*) There are no general price changes during the life of the ship.
(*j*) There are no relative price changes during the life of the ship.
(*k*) There are no productivity changes during the life of the ship.
(*l*) The owners finance the ship from their own resources.
(*m*) The owners have profits from other sources sufficient to enable them to take immediate advantage of the free depreciation allowance.

CALCULATIONS

(*a*) *Positive cash flow*

This is simply the £520,000 p.a. specified in assumption (*b*) constant throughout (because it is being maintained in real terms) suitably adjusted by lay-up periods for surveys and by the scrap value.

TABLE 5.A2. *The effect of surveys on positive cash flow*

Year (1)	Normal positive component of cash flow (£) (2)	Reduction for survey periods (£) (3)	Positive component of cash flow adjusted for surveys (£) (4) = (2)−(3)
1	520,000	Nil	520,000
2	520,000	Nil	520,000
3	520,000	Nil	520,000
4	520,000	Nil	520,000
5	520,000	Nil	520,000
6	520,000	Nil	520,000
7	520,000	Nil	520,000
8	520,000	Nil	520,000
9	520,000	Nil	520,000
10	520,000	Nil	520,000
11	520,000	Nil	520,000
12	520,000	Nil	520,000
13	520,000	51,300	468,700
14	520,000	Nil	520,000
15	520,000	Nil	520,000
16	520,000	Nil	520,000
17	520,000	102,600	417,400
18	520,000	Nil	520,000
19	520,000	Nil	520,000
20	520,000	Nil	520,000
21	520,000	153,900	366,100
22	520,000	Nil	520,000
23	520,000	Nil	520,000
24	520,000	Nil	520,000
25	582,500	Nil	582,500
26	Nil	Nil	Nil

(*b*) *Negative cash flow (before tax)*

This is simply the £360,000 p.a. specified in assumption (*c*) plus the survey costs.

TABLE 5.A3. *The effect of surveys on negative cash flow*

Year (1)	Normal negative component of cash flow (£) (2)	Survey costs (£) (3)	Negative component of cash flow adjusted for surveys (£) (4) = (2)+(3)
1	360,000	Nil	360,000
2	360,000	Nil	360,000
3	360,000	Nil	360,000
4	360,000	Nil	360,000
5	360,000	10,000	370,000
6	360,000	Nil	360,000
7	360,000	Nil	360,000
8	360,000	Nil	360,000
9	360,000	20,000	380,000
10	360,000	Nil	360,000
11	360,000	Nil	360,000
12	360,000	Nil	360,000
13	360,000	40,000	400,000
14	360,000	Nil	360,000
15	360,000	Nil	360,000
16	360,000	Nil	360,000
17	360,000	70,000	430,000
18	360,000	Nil	360,000
19	360,000	Nil	360,000
20	360,000	Nil	360,000
21	360,000	100,000	460,000
22	360,000	Nil	360,000
23	360,000	Nil	360,000
24	360,000	Nil	360,000
25	360,000	Nil	360,000
26	Nil	Nil	Nil

TABLE 5.A4. *Calculation of net present value of revenue, operating costs, corporation tax, investment grant, free depreciation and initial cost*

	Before tax			After tax		
	Positive cash flow	Negative cash flow	Net cash flow	Net cash flow	Discount factor	Discounted cash flows
Year	(£)	(£)	(£)	(£)		(£)
(1)	(2)	(3)	(4)	(5)	(6)	(7)
i	Table 5.A2	Table 5.A3	(2)−(3)	0·63860 (4)	$(1+0·07)^{-i}$	(5)×(6)
1	520,000	360,000	160,000	102,177	0·934579	95·492
2	520,000	360,000	160,000	102,177	0·873439	89,245
3	520,000	360,000	160,000	102,177	0·816298	83,407
4	520,000	360,000	160,000	102,177	0·762895	77,950
5	520,000	370,000	150,000	95,791	0,712986	68,298
6	520,000	360,000	160,000	102,177	0·666342	68,085
7	520,000	360,000	160,000	102,177	0·622750	63,631
8	520,000	360,000	160,000	102,177	0·582009	59,468
9	520,000	380,000	140,000	89,405	0·543934	48,630
10	520,000	360,000	160,000	102,177	0·508349	51,942
11	520,000	360,000	160,000	102,177	0·475093	48,544
12	520,000	360,000	160,000	102,177	0·444012	45,368
13	468,700	400,000	68,700	43,872	0·414964	18,205
14	520,000	360,000	160,000	102,177	0·387817	39·626
15	520,000	360,000	160,000	102,177	0·362446	37,034
16	520,000	360,000	160,000	102,177	0·338735	34,611
17	417,400	430,000	−12,600	−8,046	0·316574	−2,547
18	520,000	360,000	160,000	102,177	0·295864	30,230
19	520,000	360,000	160,000	102,177	0·276508	28,253
20	520,000	360,000	160,000	102,177	0·258419	26,404
21	366,100	460,000	−93,900	−59,965	0·241513	−14,482
22	520,000	360,000	160,000	102,177	0·225713	23,063
23	520,000	360,000	160,000	102,177	0·210947	21,554
24	520,000	360,000	160,000	102,177	0·197147	20,144
25	582,500	360,000	222,500	142,089	0·184249	26,180

Total 1,088,335
Plus PV of investment grant   = 0·18070 of £1,250,000 =   225,875
Plus PV of depreciation allowance = 0·28912 of £1,250,000 =   361,396

1,675,606
Less initial cost 1,260,000

Net present value £415,606

Notes: (*a*) 0·63860 in the heading of col. (5) is the Factor E from Table 5.5.
(*b*) PV of investment grant is from Table 5.1.
(*c*) PV of depreciation allowance is the Factor D from Table 5.4.

(c) *Tax*

For the 'full-tax' and 'no-tax' positions described in the body of the paper, the calculations in Table 5.4 (present value of free depreciation allowance) and 5.5 (net of corporation tax Factor E) can be used. For any other tax positions fresh calculations may be needed. In all circumstances, however, Table 5.1 (present value of investment grant) and 5.2 (capital cost after allowing for present value of investment grant) can be used. The 'full-tax' position is assumed above; accordingly, full use is made of these tables, assuming as in the earlier paper, a discount rate of 7 % throughout. (This is in contrast to the body of this paper, which assumes 6 % throughout because it has been found that this rate is more widely acceptable. 7 % is presented in this Appendix because it was used in the earlier paper.)

It will be observed that, with the aid of these short-cut methods, the whole of the rest of the NPV calculation can be reduced from four tables to one.

APPENDIX 2

INTRODUCTION

In the paper no change was allowed for in the rate of investment grant and, since this has just been increased (see Hansard, 1 Dec. 1966, p. 638, col. 1) from the 20 % embodied in this paper to 25 %, it seems appropriate to present additional calculations on the basis which will be applicable to capital payments made between 1 January 1967 and 31 December 1968 for ships, their equipment and up to three sets of containers per ship. Apart from this change, these re-calculations will be on the same quantitative assumptions and bases as before. They will employ the same notation.

The present value of a 25 % investment grant, payable with a 1½ year lag, discounting at 6 %, and referred to as 'Factor B', is:

$$B = [1 - G_N(1+r)^{-1}]C_0 = 0.77092C_0.$$

THE 'NO-TAX' POSITION

Constant improvements in net cash flow

The minimum improvement in net cash flow necessary to justify a known capital expenditure for a shipowner in this position is defined by:

$$A_{\min} = \frac{C_0 B}{\left[\dfrac{1-(1+r)^{-n}}{r}\right]} = 0\cdot06721 C_0.$$

Thus, for example, if we proposed to spend £1,000 on a ship with a life-expectancy of 20 years, and if this expenditure ranks for investment grant at 25 %, it will require on these assumptions an improvement in net cash flow of *at least* £67 p.a. to justify it. Conversely, an improvement in net cash flow of £100 would justify a *maximum* capital expenditure on these assumptions of £1,488.

Geometric improvements in net cash flow

If the improvement in net cash flow is expected to increase geometrically (as it might if it were derived from a saving in the wages bill) and at 3 % p.a. then:

$$A_{1\min} = \frac{C_0 B}{\left[\dfrac{1-\left(\dfrac{1+g}{1+r}\right)^{n}}{r-g}\right]} = 0\cdot52943 C_0.$$

Thus, for example, if we propose to spend £1,000 on a ship with a life expectancy of 20 years, if the expenditure ranks for investment grant at 25 % and if the resulting improvement in net cash flow is expected to increase at 3 % p.a. then it will require, on these assumptions, an *initial* improvement in net cash flow of *at least* £53 to justify it. Conversely, an initial improvement in net cash flow of £100 would justify, on these assumptions, a *maximum* capital expenditure of £1,889.

Ready-reckoners 3 and 4 show the equivalents of these answers for various sums. Ready-reckoner 3A shows as the left-hand figure on each line the net capital cost change equivalent, on these assumptions, to the constant improvement in net cash flow shown in the stub.

Ready-reckoner 3B shows, again as the left-hand figure on each line, the net capital cost change equivalent, on these assumptions, to the improvement in net cash flow whose initial value is shown in the stub and which increases at 3 % p.a. thereafter. Ready-reckoner 4 shows the converse to both of these: 4A shows as the left-hand figure on each line the constant net cash flow improvement equivalent to the net capital cost changes shown in the stub; 4B shows, still as the left-hand figure on each line, the initial net cash flow improvement, increasing thereafter at 3 % p.a., equivalent to the net capital cost change shown in the stub.

THE 'FULL-TAX' POSITION

The adjustment ('Factor D') to allow for free depreciation is now:

$$D = (1 - G_N) t(1+r)^{-1} C_0 = 0.27489 C_0.$$

The adjustment ('Factor E') to allow for the corporation tax remains:

$$E = 1 - t(1+r)^{-1} = 0.63349 A.$$

Constant improvements in net cash flow

The result of these is that, if we calculate on the full-tax basis, the minimum (constant) improvement in net cash flow necessary to justify a known capital expenditure is:

$$A_{\min} = \frac{C_0 B - C_0 D}{E \left[\dfrac{1 - (1+r)^{-n}}{r} \right]} = 0.06827 C_0.$$

Thus, if we propose to spend £1,000 on a ship with a life-expectancy of 20 years, and if this expenditure ranks for investment grant at 25 %, it will require, on these assumptions, an improvement in net cash flow of *at least* £68 to justify it. Conversely, an improvement in net cash flow of £100 would justify a *maximum* capital expenditure, on these assumptions, of £1,465.

Geometric improvements in net cash flow

If the improvement in net cash flow is expected to increase geometrically at 3 % p.a. then:

$$A_{1\,min} = \frac{C_0 B - C_0 D}{E\left[\dfrac{1-\left(\dfrac{1+g}{1+r}\right)^n}{r-g}\right]} = 0\cdot5377 C_0.$$

Thus, if we propose to spend £1,000 on a ship with a life-expectancy of 20 years, and if the expenditure ranks for investment grant at 25 %, and if the resulting improvement in net cash flow is expected to increase at 3 % p.a. then it will require, on these assumptions, an *initial* improvement in net cash flow of *at least* £54 to justify it. Conversely, an initial improvement in net cash flow of £100 would justify on these assumptions, a *maximum* capital expenditure of £1,860.

Ready-reckoners 3 and 4 show the equivalents of these answers for various sums. Ready-reckoner 3 A shows, as the right-hand figure on each line, the net capital cost changes equivalent on the full-tax assumptions given above, to the constant improvements in net cash flow shown in the stub. Ready-reckoner 3 B shows, as the right-hand figure on each line, the net capital cost changes equivalent on these assumptions to the improvement in net cash flow whose initial value is shown in the stub and which increases at 3 % p.a. thereafter. Ready-reckoner 4 shows the converse of both of these. 4 A shows, as the right-hand figure on each line, the constant net cash flow improvement equivalent to the net capital cost changes shown in the stub. 4 B shows, again as the right-hand figure on each line, the initial net cash flow improvement, increasing thereafter at 3 % p.a., equivalent to the net capital cost change shown on the stub.

Ready-reckoner 3 A: Solution of net capital cost change equivalent to known constant net cash flow change. Left-hand figure no tax, right-hand figure full tax basis.

Ready-reckoner 3 B: Solution of net capital cost change equivalent to known initial level of geometrically increasing net cash flow change. Left-hand figure no tax, right-hand figure full tax basis.

Net cash flow change (£)	3 A. Constant (tax position, £)		3 B. Geometric growth (tax position, £)	
	No-tax	Full-tax	No-tax	Full-tax
100	1,488	1,465	1,889	1,860
200	2,976	2,930	3,778	3,719
300	4,463	4,394	5,667	5,579
400	5,951	5,859	7,555	7,439
500	7,439	7,324	9,444	9,298
600	8,927	8,789	11,333	11,158
700	10,415	10,254	13,222	13,017
800	11,902	11,718	15,111	14,877
900	13,390	13,183	17,000	16,737
1,000	14,878	14,648	18,888	18,596
1,500	22,317	21,972	28,333	27,895
2,000	29,756	29,296	37,777	37,193
2,500	37,195	36,620	47,221	46,491
3,000	44,634	43,944	56,665	55,789
3,500	52,073	51,268	66,109	65,087
4,000	59,512	58,592	75,553	74,385
4,500	66,952	65,916	84,998	83,684
5,000	74,391	73,241	94,442	92,982
6,000	89,269	87,889	113,330	111,578
7,000	104,147	102,537	132,219	130,175
8,000	119,025	117,185	151,107	148,771
9,000	133,903	131,833	169,995	167,367
10,000	148,781	146,481	188,884	185,964
15,000	223,172	219,722	283,326	278,945
20,000	297,562	292,962	377,767	371,927
30,000	446,344	439,443	566,651	557,891
40,000	595,125	585,924	755,535	743,854
50,000	743,906	732,405	944,419	929,818
60,000	892,687	878,886	1,133,302	1,115,782
70,000	1,041,468	1,025,367	1,322,186	1,301,745
80,000	1,190,250	1,171,848	1,511,070	1,487,709
90,000	1,339,031	1,318,329	1,699,953	1,673,672
100,000	1,487,812	1,464,811	1,888,837	1,859,636

N.B. Linear interpolation may be made vertically: not horizontally.

Ready-reckoner 4A: Solution of net cash flow change equivalent to known constant net capital cost change. Left-hand figure no-tax, right-hand figure full-tax basis.

Ready-reckoner 4B: Solution of net cash flow change equivalent to known initial level of geometrically increasing net cash flow change. Left-hand figure no-tax, right-hand figure full-tax basis.

Net capital cost charge (£)	4A. Constant (tax position, £)		4B. Geometric growth (tax position, £)	
	No-tax	Full-tax	No-tax	Full-tax
100	7	7	5	5
200	13	14	11	11
300	20	20	16	16
400	27	27	21	22
500	34	34	26	27
600	40	41	32	32
700	47	48	37	38
800	54	55	42	43
900	60	61	48	48
1,000	67	68	53	54
1,500	101	102	79	81
2,000	134	137	106	108
2,500	168	171	132	134
3,000	202	205	159	161
3,500	235	239	185	188
4,000	269	273	212	215
4,500	302	307	238	242
5,000	336	341	265	269
6,000	403	410	318	323
7,000	470	478	371	376
8,000	538	546	424	430
9,000	605	614	476	484
10,000	672	683	529	538
15,000	1,008	1,024	794	807
20,000	1,344	1,365	1,059	1,075
30,000	2,016	2,048	1,588	1,613
40,000	2,689	2,731	2,118	2,151
50,000	3,361	3,413	2,647	2,689
60,000	4,033	4,096	3,177	3,226
70,000	4,705	4,779	3,706	3,764
80,000	5,377	5,461	4,235	4,302
90,000	6,049	6,144	4,765	4,840
100,000	6,721	6,827	5.294	5.377

N.B. Linear interpolation may be made vertically: not horizontally.

6

THE TURNROUND OF CARGO LINERS AND ITS EFFECT UPON SEA TRANSPORT COSTS[1]

Introduction

It is often suggested that cargo liners spend an excessive amount of time in port and that, if this could be reduced, substantial reductions could be achieved in the cost of sea transport. The object of this paper is to test this hypothesis and to present calculations indicating the orders of magnitude involved in various combinations of route length and turnround time. Although the data and assumptions do not refer to any specific route, cargo or shipowner, they are believed to be not unreasonable for present circumstances and applicable to most competitive shipowning countries.

Basic data[2]

In order to isolate the effects of the variables being considered one ship design is assumed throughout. This is a typical modern cargo liner of:

    (*a*) 10,000 grt. (closed shelter deck).

    (*b*) 12,500 dwt. tons.

    (*c*) 16 knots with single-screw, super-charged diesel engine of 9,200 SHP, having an exhaust boiler for some auxiliary services and diesel generators for use in port and providing an overall specific fuel consumption of 0·36 lbs per SHP/hour at sea and 2 tons per day in port, both at an average of 100*s*. per ton of oil. This gives a fuel cost of £177 per day at sea and £10 per day in port.

---

[1] I am indebted to colleagues in HM Treasury, the Board of Trade, the National Ports Council and the British Transport Docks Board for commenting on earlier drafts of this paper and to HM Treasury and the Board of Trade for permission to publish it. I alone am responsible for the views expressed and for any errors and omissions.

[2] These data were published in an earlier paper: 'Investment in shipping and the balance of payments', *J. Ind. Econ.* March 1965. (Now reprinted above, pp. 46–60.)

(*d*) 650,000 cu.ft. bale capacity.

(*e*) 43 crew.

Assuming that the ship is, on average, 80 % full and makes three round voyages a year when spending 60 % of its time in port, the costs according to the usual headings are as follows:

TABLE 6.1. *The costs of a cargo liner*

	£ per day	£000 p.a.
Commissions	—	27
Cargo-handling	—	136
Fuel	—	28
Port dues, pilotage, tug hire, Customs fees, etc.	—	50
Crew wages	150	55
Crew provisions	21	8
Stores, including lubricating oil	30	11
Repairs	125	46
Insurance	55	20
Sundries	11	4
Administration	55	20
Total	£447	£405

The capital cost is £1,250,000. This is equivalent to capital charges on the basis used in this paper (see below) of £298 per day or £108,981 p.a. at a discount rate of 6 %. The conventional accounting procedure of straight-line depreciation plus 6 % interest on the mean of book values in the first and last years would give capital charges of £278 per day.[1]

[1] On the basis (5 % depreciation + 7 % on the full replacement cost of the ship) used by P. A. Lane in 'An aspect of the cost of port delays', *Yorkshire Bulletin of Economic and Social Research* (Nov. 1957), the capital charges would have been £150,000 p.a. or £411 per day. The daily cash costs in port in this paper are £447 + £212 (port charges—see below) + £10 (fuel) = £669. Martin-Jenkins and Sir Nicholas Cayzer (*op. cit.*, below), in implying or quoting daily costs of £545 and £600 respectively, would appear to have excluded capital charges altogether. The OECD publication *Maritime Transport 1963* at p. 37 suggests £670 per day for 'operating costs, depreciation and normal interest on capital' (on an unspecified basis and rate) but excluded the additional port dues included here. The figures used in this paper are thus some 12½ % greater than those assumed by OECD; this may be due to differences in the method of calculating capital charges or in the ship taken as an example.

Assumptions

(*a*) *Cargoes:* All cargoes occupy 80 % of the bale capacity at an average density (including broken stowage) of 65 cu.ft. per long ton. Each cargo is, therefore, of 8,000 long tons. If the broken stowage were 10 % there would be about 11,800 measurement tons of 40 cu.ft. in the cargo and a stowage factor, excluding broken stowage, of 59 cu.ft. per long ton.

(*b*) *Voyages:* All voyages involve two such cargoes, loading and/or discharging being carried out at two ports at each end of each passage. There are, therefore, four port calls in each (round) voyage.

(*c*) *Commissions and cargo-handling costs:* These costs do not normally vary with route length and, while cargo-handling costs might vary inversely with turnround times (e.g. if shift premia or different techniques were employed), they are assumed constant here in order to isolate the effects of varying one voyage component at a time. Since the data in Table 6.1 refer to 6 cargoes of 8,000 long tons each, it follows that commissions cost £0·565 and cargo-handling £2·833 per long ton.

(*d*) *Port charges:* Exit and entry costs (e.g. tug hire, pilotage and linesmen) are assumed to cost £300 per port call. With 12 port calls per year this leaves £46,400 p.a. to be accounted for by other port charges, e.g. tonnage dues payable by the ship. If all of this represents tonnage dues it is equivalent to 5·088*d.* per g.r.t./day or £212 per day in port. This last figure is equivalent to a daily berth-rent. It may appear high in relation to some current price levels, but it must be remembered that these reflect only the general practice among port authorities of attempting to raise sufficient revenue to defray their cash costs (including explicit interest charges) plus depreciation, and that depreciation is only sometimes on a replacement cost basis.

(*e*) *Repair costs and periods:* Ships are subject to quinquennial surveys by classification societies, and these are of increasing severity. A given ship's time-stream of net cash flows thus tends to be extremely uneven, partly because of the increased repair costs and partly because of the (necessarily simultaneous) fall in revenue. (The earlier surveys can be carried out without interrupting the ship's trading and thus without reducing revenue: the later ones cannot.) Given the type of ship and assuming the latest technical standards, it is reasonable to assume that repair costs are not significantly affected by changes in route length or turnround times. User cost is ignored here, partly because reliable evidence is not available and partly because it appears to have both positive and negative elements. The positive element is the increased wear and tear on cargo-handling gear (principally derrick runners and blocks), the increased damage to the ship's holds and hatchways and the increased engine-hours per year associated with greater annual carryings. The negative element is the reduced underwater fouling which results from shorter stays in port. This treatment is only one of a number of points on which the approach adopted here differs from that of P. A. Lane.[1] For comparative purposes, therefore, the level of repair costs and of repair periods may be assumed to be constant over the ship's life. This will, however, slightly reduce the validity of the absolute levels of cost shown later.

(*f*) *Life of the ship:* This is assumed to be 20 years. The results of this paper would not be significantly affected if a life of 25 years were assumed.

(*g*) *Opportunity cost of capital:* This, the rate of return that might reasonably be expected in the next best alternative investment, is crucial to such calculations; without it the rate of return above which investors may reasonably be expected to order ships, and below which they may reasonably be expected to cease ordering them, cannot be defined. An assumption on this cannot be avoided, and must refer to a rate net of taxes, etc., and in real terms. Partly because there is some doubt as to the opportunity cost of capital and partly to test the sensitivity of such calculations as these to small variations in it, two rates will be assumed here: 6 and 8 %. As this concept refers to the returns likely to be made on other investments than shipping, neither of these figures has any necessary relation to the rates of return, internal or on capital employed, obtained in shipping over any particular period.

(*h*) *Demand:* It is assumed that cargoes will continue to be available at the same freight rates even though the effective annual

---

[1] P. A. Lane, *op. cit.*, assumed one-third of repair costs varied with the level of activity but did not mention the negative element of user cost. His paper was an analysis of historical variations in turnround of cargo liners in the UK/ Australia trade.

carrying capacity of the ship is increased. The validity of this assumption will be discussed on page 148.

Preliminary calculations

(a) *Cargo* per round voyage = 16,000 long tons

(b) *Cost per cargo* per round voyage
Commissions 16,000 tons at £0·563 = £ 9,008
Stevedoring 16,000 tons at £2·833 = £45,328
Exit and⎫
Entry ⎬ 4 calls at £300   = £ 1,200
charges⎭

Total cash cost for cargo per round voyage = £55,536

(c) *Cost per day at sea*
Cash operating costs at   £447
Bunkers at   £177

Total cash cost per day at sea   = £   624

(d) *Cost per day in port*
Cash operating costs at =   £447
Bunkers at   £ 10
Port charges at   £212

Total cash cost per day in port   = £   669

Methods[1]

A shipowner will tend to build ships if and when he thinks that it will be profitable for him to do so; and this depends, among other things,

---

[1] The methods adopted here contrast with those of R. L. Marris in his recent book: *The economics of capital utilisation* (Cambridge, 1964) in three principal ways. First, Marris uses private profit rather than the concept of social cost as measured by shadow price; but if every firm adopts new, profitable techniques (and there seems no very good reason why it should not) then prices and profits will be competed down to a 'normal' level. The reduction in social costs will remain: nor is it represented by the difference in the profit rate caused by prices being competed downwards. Secondly, Marris seems content with using crude rates of return to indicate the optimal choice amongst alternative proposals. Thirdly, this paper is not concerned solely with *capital* utilisation: when a ship is used more intensively in port there are associated reductions in the average costs (per ton of cargo delivered) of the crew, fuel, repairs, stores, insurance and administration.

on the level of freight rates. The profitability of a proposed ship may be expressed in terms of its net present value, or the excess of the discounted net cash flows over the capital cost of the ship.[1] This may be expressed mathematically as

$$\text{NPV} = \sum_{i=1}^{i=n} [A_i(1+r)^{-i}] - C_0,$$

where i is a year of the ship's life

n is the total life of the ship

A is the net cash flow (i.e. the excess of cash revenue over cash costs)

r is the opportunity cost of capital and

C_0 is the initial cost of the ship.

The cash flow may be taken either before or after taxes, etc. But it has been shown earlier that, conveniently, the present value of corporation tax and tax allowances taken together is, for British shipping, approximately zero.[2] In the subsequent calculations taxes and tax allowances will be ignored. As far as the calculations in this paper are concerned, investment grants are also ignored, but this makes little difference to the results—certainly less than the difference between using discount rates of 6 % and 8 %. Alternatively, the calculations may be regarded as being in social rather than private terms.

Because we are assuming that repair costs and periods are constant over the ship's life, and because there seems no obvious reason to suppose that any other cost items will vary sufficiently, or with sufficient predictability, to affect the conclusions, we may assume that the net cash flow time stream is flat. This enables us to simplify our formula to:

$$\text{NPV} = A\left[\frac{1-(1+r)^{-n}}{r}\right] - C_0.$$

Values of $\left[\dfrac{1-(1+r)^{-n}}{r}\right]$ may, of course, be obtained from annuity tables.

---

[1] For a further discussion of this subject in a shipping context see R. O. Goss: 'Economic criteria for optimal ship design', *Trans. R. Instn Nav. Archit.* Oct. 1965 reprinted above, pp. 61–99. In a general context the subject has been covered in a number of recent works.   [2] See above, p. 114.

Where $r = 6\%$ and $n = 20$ years, the value is $11\cdot4699$, and where $r = 8\%$ and $n = 20$ years, it is $9\cdot81815$.

The net flow expression A may, of course, be expanded into $(R_c - C_c)$, where R_c is the gross (cash) revenue and C_c the cash costs for a year. The assumptions given above are sufficient to calculate C_c for any desired combination of circumstances. The revenue expression R_c may in turn be expanded into $(P \times Q)$ where Q represents the tonnage of cargo carried in a year (for which the above assumptions are also sufficient) and P represents the freight rate.

It is, therefore, possible to rewrite the equation as:

$$\text{NPV} = (PQ - C_c)\left[\frac{1-(1+r)^{-n}}{r}\right] - C_0$$

and to solve it for the freight rate which is equivalent to the assumed internal rate of return by assuming NPV = zero and transposing it into:

$$P = \frac{1}{Q}\left(\frac{C_0}{\left[\dfrac{1-(1+r)^{-n}}{r}\right]} + C_c\right)$$

for which values may easily be calculated.

The values of P thus produced may be termed the 'shadow price' of using the given ship in the given circumstances. This measure takes into account the operating costs concerned, the capital cost of the ship (thus any inclusion of depreciation would involve double-counting), the rate of return expected in the long run and the quantities of cargo concerned. It may be noted that, if sufficient data on repair costs and periods were available, it would be possible to relax the assumption of Q and C_c being constant by solving the formula:

$$C_0 = \sum_{i=1}^{i=n}(PQ_i - C_{ci})(1+r)^{-i}$$

for P by trial and error.

It is, in other words, possible to calculate a shadow price which takes account, not only of those costs mentioned in the preceding paragraph and assumed in this paper to be constant over the ship's life, but also of any specified variations in these costs over the life of the ship. Moreover, it is also possible to consider the effects of any specified variations in the level of output over the life of the ship. As noted above, however, this is likely to affect the absolute levels of the shadow prices rather than comparisons made between them for the purposes of this paper.

To recapitulate the argument thus far: Whether or not the time stream of net cash flows is flat, it is reasonable to assume that, at any freight rate above the shadow price as defined above, the higher rate of return obtainable by investment in ships will bring forth an increased supply of ships, whereupon competition will bring the rate down again. Conversely, at any rate below P, shipowners will be less willing to order ships, the supply of ships will be reduced and the rate will rise again. P is therefore the long-term equilibrium rate about which market rates will tend to fluctuate and towards which, with given techniques, they will have a long-term tendency to move. Given the competitive nature of the shipping industry and the ability of outsiders to compete their way into shipping conferences, such differences are also likely to indicate differences in the general level of freight rates. The length of the time lags involved in correcting imbalances in world supply and demand for ships (the slump which started in 1957, for example, did not begin to end till 1963) might, however, delay the appearance of such effects. It should not be inferred from these calculations that there is anything 'just' about these levels of freight rate, or that there is anything 'unjust' about any other level. Market rates must always reflect the world supply-demand position of shipping (and also the distortions caused by national policies of, e.g. flag discrimination and subsidies).

Results

Calculations have been made on:
(a) Round voyage distances of 5,000, 10,000, 15,000 and 20,000 nautical miles, and
(b) turnround times involving 0, 10, 20, 30, 40, 50, 60, 70 and 80 % of the year being spent in port.
The shadow prices thus obtained are shown in Table 6.2.

TABLE 6.2. *Variations in the shadow prices of cargo-liner services with route length and turnround times*

% of year spent		Round voyage distance, n.m.							
		5,000		10,000		15,000		20,000	
in port	at sea	6%	8%	6%	8%	6%	8%	6%	8%
		£	£	£	£	£	£	£	£
80	20	7·37	7·57	11·26	11·67	15·15	15·77	19·05	19·86
70	30	6·05	6·19	8·64	8·91	11·22	11·63	13·79	14·33
60	40	5·40	5·50	7·33	7·53	9·26	9·56	11·18	11·59
50	50	5·01	5·09	6·54	6·71	8·08	8·32	9·61	9·94
40	60	4·75	4·81	6·02	6·15	7·29	7·50	8·57	8·84
30	70	4·56	4·62	5·64	5·75	6·73	6·90	7·82	8·05
20	80	4·42	4·47	5·36	5·47	6·31	6·47	7·26	7·46
10	90	4·31	4·35	5·15	5·24	5·98	6·12	6·82	7·00
0	100	4·22	4·26	4·97	5·05	5·72	5·84	6·47	6·63

Some of the principal results of this calculation are already clear:

(*a*) the shadow price is not very sensitive to changes in the opportunity cost of capital;

(*b*) the shadow price is sensitive to changes in the proportion of time spent in port, particularly on the longer routes;

(*c*) the shadow price appears to be very sensitive to changes in the round voyage distance, particularly when the proportion of time spent in port is high. This, however, is not a fair test, since, with a constant *proportion* (rather than a constant absolute amount of time) in port, increasing distance is associated, in Tables 6.2 and 6.3, with increasing periods not only at sea but also in port. Accordingly, comparisons should be made between the lines of these tables rather than between the columns.

More detailed results of the same calculations, showing round voyages p.a., port, sea and total days per round voyage, output (i.e. tons carried p.a.) and cost per ton-mile, are shown in Table 6.3. The implied rates of cargo handling, in tons per gross port day (i.e. including weekends and public holidays) are shown in Table 6.4.

The most important results of these calculations lie not so much in the absolute as in the proportionate changes of the shadow prices.

TABLE 6.3. *Round voyages p.a., port, sea and total days p.r.v., annual carryings and cost per ton-mile for various combinations of turnround and r.v. distance*

	Percentage of year		Round voyage distance, n.m.			
	in port	at sea	5,000	10,000	15,000	20,000
Round voyages p.a.			8·4	4·2	2·8	2·1
Port days p.r.v.			30	61	91	121
Sea days p.r.v.			13	26	39	52
Total days p.r.v.	70	30	43	87	130	173
Tons carried p.a.			134875	67357	44924	33759
Cost per ton-mile (£)			0·00242	0·00173	0·00150	0·00138
Round voyages p.a.			11·2	5·6	3·7	2·8
Port days p.r.v.			19½	39	58½	78
Sea days p.r.v.			13	26	39	52
Total days p.r.v.	60	40	32½	65	97½	130
Tons carried p.a.			179690	89826	59896	44931
Cost per ton-mile (£)			0·00216	0·00147	0·00123	0·00112
Round voyages p.a.			14	7	4·7	3·5
Port days p.r.v.			13	26	39	52
Sea days p.r.v.			13	26	39	52
Total days p.r.v.	50	50	26	52	78	104
Tons carried p.a.			224614	112307	74872	56155
Cost per ton-mile (£)			0·00200	0·00131	0·00108	0·00096
Round voyages p.a.			16·8	8·4	5·6	4·2
Port days p.r.v.			9	17	26	35
Sea days p.r.v.			13	26	39	52
Total days p.r.v.	40	60	22	43	65	87
Tons carried p.a.			269125	134875	89845	67357
Cost per ton-mile (£)			0·00190	0·00120	0·00097	0·00086
Round voyages p.a.			19·6	9·9	6·6	4·9
Port days p.r.v.			6	11	17	22
Sea days p.r.v.			13	26	39	52
Total days p.r.v.	30	70	19	37	56	74
Tons carried p.a.			313980	157837	104846	78599
Cost per ton-mile (£)			0·00182	0·00113	0·00090	0·00078
Round voyages p.a.			22·4	11·2	7·5	5·6
Port days p.r.v.			3	6½	10	13
Sea days p.r.v.			13	26	39	52
Total days p.r.v.	20	80	16	32½	49	65
Tons carried p.a.			358284	179693	119673	89845
Cost per ton-mile (£)			0·00177	0·00107	0·00084	0·00073
Round voyages p.a.			25·3	12·6	8·4	6·3
Port days p.r.v.			1½	3	4	6
Sea days p.r.v.			13	26	39	52
Total days p.r.v.	10	90	14½	29	43	58
Tons carried p.a.			405555	202075	134875	101039
Cost per ton-mile (£)			0·00172	0·00103	0·00080	0·00068

TABLE 6.4. *Tonnage of cargo handled per gross port-day*

% of year		Round voyage distance, n.m.			
in port	at sea	5,000	10,000	15,000	20,000
80	20	308	154	103	77
70	30	533	262	176	132
60	40	821	410	274	205
50	50	1,231	615	410	308
40	60	1,778	941	615	457
30	70	2,667	1,455	941	727
20	80	5,333	2,462	1,600	1,231
10	90	10,667	5,333	4,000	2,667

These changes can be observed by plotting on a graph, or by calculating, the proportionate change in shadow price resulting from reducing the proportion of time spent in port. Figure 1 shows the whole of the data presented in Table 6.2. Figure 2*a* repeats the shadow prices for a 10,000 n.m. round voyage and shows how each is comprised. Figure 2*b* again repeats the shadow prices and adds the various supplementary results of Table 6.3. In Figures 1 and 2*b* the shadow price calculated by discounting at 6 % is shown by a continuous line, while the accompanying broken line gives that obtained by calculating at 8 %.

The proportionate changes in shadow prices resulting from altering the proportion of time spent in port are shown in Tables 6.5*a* (for 5,000 n.m.), 6.5*b* (for 10,000 n.m.), 6.5*c* (for 15,000 n.m.) and 6.5*d* (for 20,000 n.m.). Each of these tables may be read in the same way as a distance table, by entering at the top with the higher of the two proportions of time in port and taking that figure from the body of the table which lies in the appropriate column and in the line opposite the lower proportion of time spent in port. By reversing the process the tables may also be used for the effects of increasing the proportion of time spent in port.

It is possible to restate these findings in terms of the change in the shadow price for each day spent in port. A reduction of one day in port time, on the basis of calculation employed in this paper and regardless of route length, reduces the shadow price by about £0·121 per long ton.

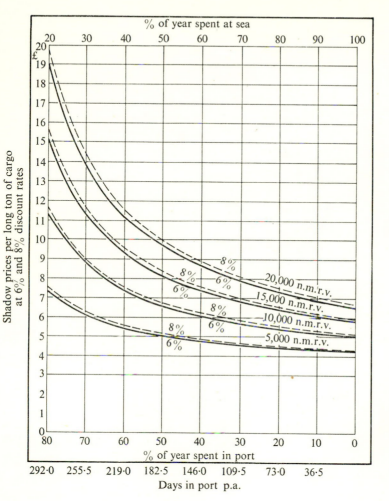

Figure 1

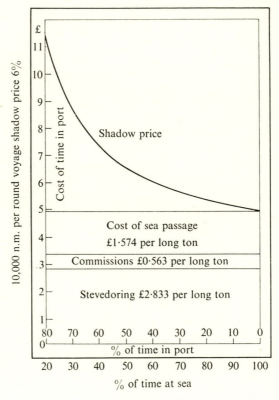

Figure 2*a*

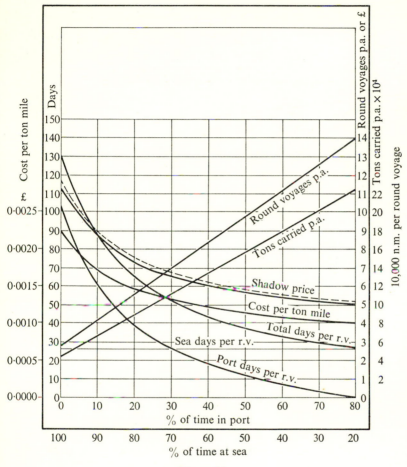

Figure 2*b*

TABLE 6.5. *Change in shadow price with change (6 % basis) in turnround*

% of time in port	80	70	60	50	40	30	20	10	0
(a) Percentage reduction on 5,000 n.m. r.v.									
80	0								
70	17·9	0							
60	26·7	10·7	0						
50	32·0	17·2	7·2	0					
40	35·5	21·5	12·0	5·2	0				
30	38·1	24·6	15·6	9·0	4·0	0			
20	40·0	26·9	18·1	11·8	6·9	3·1	0		
10	41·5	28·8	20·2	14·0	9·3	5·5	2·5	0	
0	42·7	30·2	21·9	15·8	11·2	7·5	4·5	2·1	0
(b) Percentage reduction on 10,000 n.m. r.v.									
80	0								
70	23·3	0							
60	34·9	15·2	0						
50	41·9	24·3	10·8	0					
40	46·5	30·3	17·9	8·0	0				
30	49·9	34·7	23·1	13·8	6·3	0			
20	52·4	38·0	26·9	18·0	11·0	5·0	0		
10	54·3	40·4	29·7	21·3	14·5	8·7	3·9	0	
0	55·9	42·5	32·2	24·0	17·4	11·9	7·3	3·5	0
(c) Percentage reduction on 15,000 n.m r.v.									
80	0								
70	25·9	0							
60	38·9	17·5	0						
50	46·7	28·0	12·7	0					
40	51·9	35·0	21·3	9·8	0				
30	55·6	40·0	27·3	16·7	7·7	0			
20	58·3	43·8	31·9	21·9	13·4	6·2	0		
10	60·5	46·7	35·4	26·0	18·0	11·1	5·2	0	
0	62·2	49·0	38·2	29·2	21·5	15·0	9·4	4·3	0
(d) Percentage reduction on 20,000 n.m. r.v.									
80	0								
70	27·6	0							
60	41·3	18·9	0						
50	49·6	30·3	14·0	0					
40	55·0	37·9	23·3	10·8	0				
30	59·0	43·3	30·1	18·6	8·8	0			
20	61·9	47·4	35·1	24·5	15·3	7·2	0		
10	64·2	50·5	39·0	29·0	20·4	12·8	6·1	0	
0	66·0	53·1	42·1	32·7	24·5	17·3	10·9	5·1	0

Conclusions

It is obvious from the foregoing that changes in turnround times exert a marked effect upon the cost of sea transport by cargo liner. The available evidence,[1] admittedly sparse (for there are no regularly published statistics of this important determinant of ship efficiency), suggests that cargo liners commonly spend about 60 % of their time in port, and the near-unanimity of the cited references on this point is impressive.

The reference to New Zealand also suggests that, at least in that country, only 15 % of the total time in port was occupied in working cargo; the remainder consisted of weekends, nights when cargo was not being worked and periods spent awaiting a berth, awaiting cargo or suffering from breakdown (and in roughly that order of importance). Moreover, this 15 % refers to 'winch time'—i.e. when cargo is being worked at *any* hatch in the ship. Since cargo liners have several hatches, a proportion of this 15 % must refer to periods when the cargo-handling ability of the ship was being used well below capacity. (Facilities are much the same at each hatch, and adjacent hatches do not normally interfere with one another; thus the law of diminishing returns does not apply in this context, at least up to the point when all hatches are being worked at full straight time.) If we assumed that this 15 % winch time is equivalent to 10 % of full capacity cargo-working, it would follow that, while 60 % of the ship's time was spent in port, only 6 % of the year was spent in loading and discharging cargo at full-capacity cargo-handling equivalent. In other words, half

---

[1] See, e.g. *U.N. Monthly Bulletin of Statistics*, Sept. 1954 (64·4 %); OEEC Maritime Transport Committee *Annual Report* 1954 (58·9 %); R. M. Thwaites: 'The economics of ship time', *Trans. NE Cst Instn Engrs and Shipbldrs*, Jan. 1959 (60 %), from which figures were taken for the *Report of the Committee of Inquiry into the major ports of Great Britain* (Rochdale Report) Cmnd. 1824, 1962, at p. 112; Producers' Boards Shipping Utilisation Committee and New Zealand Trade Streamlining Committee: *New Zealand overseas trade; report on shipping, ports, transport and other services*, New Zealand and London, 1964, para. 97 (56·4 to 61·2 %); Speech by D. F. Martin-Jenkins reported in the *Chamber of Shipping of the UK Annual Report* 1965/6 (59·1 %) and speech by Sir Nicholas Cayzer to the 11th AGM of the British & Commonwealth Shipping Co. Ltd on 27 July 1966 (58 %). Lane (*op. cit.*) cites figures for the Australia–UK trade of 65·7 % for 1951 and 59·1 % for 1955. Only a small proportion of this is occupied in going into and out of port or in delays caused by weather.

TABLE 6.6. *Reductions in shadow price by reducing time in port from* 60 *to* 20 %

Round voyage distance (n.m.)	Reduction in shadow price (%)
5,000	18·1
10,000	26·9
15,000	31·9
20,000	35·1

The (unweighted) average of the reductions shown in Table 6.6 is 28 %.

the average ship's life was spent doing nothing in particular, and the largest single reason for this was the limitations on actual working hours.

It follows that, even allowing for a certain amount of wasted time, it is quite possible that the 60 % of the year now spent in port by the average cargo liner could be reduced to 20 %,[1] thus doubling its annual carrying capacity. The resulting reductions in shadow prices (from Tables 6.5a, b, c and d) are shown in Table 6.6.

It was assumed earlier that cargoes would continue to be available at the same freight rates. If the effect of faster turnround was that the ships in question were laid up, there would be no saving of capital costs and the calculations of shadow prices presented here would be misleading. But we can reasonably assume that the more efficient use of a ship or ships on one route displaces the least efficient ship employed anywhere into lay-up. (Ships are generally marginal substitutes for one another, except that dry cargo carriers are not substitutes for tankers—an irrelevant point in the present context.) The

[1] A pre-war example of remarkable success in this field was referred to by the late W. MacGillivray in 'Speed at sea and despatch in port', *Trans. Instn Nav. Archit.* July 1948, where he recorded how, because of a breakdown, three ships had maintained a service which normally required four, and had continued doing so for some months. Three-shift working was adopted and some 14,000 tons of cargo, were on many occasions, handled in three days. This included time spent in shifting berth, and may, therefore, be regarded as equivalent to about 5,000 tons per day. This rate, which was achieved with ships built in 1929, is much higher than all the rates implied in this paper at proportions of time in port in excess of 10 %, except on the 5,000 n.m. route.

least efficient ship employed (the marginal ship) will be making negligible gross profits[1] and, therefore, will have running costs equal to the sum of an intra-marginal ship's costs and whatever gross profits that intra-marginal ship is making minus the (negligible) lay-up costs of the marginal ship. Assuming ships to be at least marginally mobile between routes, the savings to be obtained for improving turnround are therefore real resource savings, and in practice these resources (e.g. the seamen) have alternative employments. This assumption would become invalid only if there were so remarkable *and unexpected* an improvement in turnround times (e.g. on many routes at the same time) as to affect the general supply/demand position of world shipping (e.g. by precipitating a large increase in laid-up tonnage).

The shadow price reductions shown in Table 6.6, of course, take no account of any increases in factor prices which might result from more intensive working. It is entirely possible, however, that any extension of working hours would lead to higher earnings (it is probable that shift-working by the dock labour employed in cargo handling would only be undertaken in exchange for significantly increased earnings to compensate for the disruption of home life and leisure activities). It would then be necessary to consider whether the net effect of improving turnround on the one hand and of experiencing higher dock labour costs on the other hand is still a reduction in shadow price and, if so, how great that reduction would be. Unless multiple shift working led to a significant reduction in productivity (i.e. tons of cargo handled per man-hour)—this is perhaps unlikely because current working hours often contain a great deal of overtime and, with the hard physical effort involved in break-bulk cargo-handling techniques, it is doubtful whether any greater tonnage is handled in a man-day of ten hours than in one of eight hours—or unless the reduction in shadow prices led to a reduction in freight rates sufficient to increase the quantity of goods transported by sea, there would be no need to alter the size of the labour force employed.[2]

---

[1] Compare Shotaro Kojima: 'The effects of shipping competition on freight rates', *Kyoto Univ. Econ. Rev.* July 1927 and A. Strømme Svendsen: 'Factors determining the laying-up of ships', *Shipbuilding and Shipping Record*, 19 June 1958.

[2] Fewer berths would be needed for the same annual throughput of cargo at the port; thus work could be concentrated on the most efficient berths. For an expanding cargo throughput less capital investment would be needed.

But the reductions in shadow prices shown in Table 6.6 are so great that, although the largest single item in the present structure of costs (as divided into the conventional shipping accountancy headings shown earlier) is cargo-handling, and although this consists largely of wages, almost incredibly large shift premia would be necessary to negate those reductions.

Multi-shift working (and it should not be supposed that this is the only way of improving the turnround of cargo liners) may, of course, lead to difficulties in warehousing and inland transport. Railways often operate continuously but at most general cargo ports only a minor proportion of liner cargo now arrives or departs by rail. Road transport is much more difficult to operate continuously, and even if this could be arranged it would be impossible to allow for continuous departures from, or arrivals at, inland points unless the originators or recipients of the cargo themselves worked multiple shifts. This is primarily a problem of coping with short-term lags and bottlenecks; it obviously warrants further study of, for example, the opportunities of organizing modern sorting, warehousing and calling-forward techniques and facilities, so that the delays in transfer of cargo between inland transport and dockside do not impede the more rapid transfer of cargo between ship and quay.

This paper has considered no more than the effects on shadow prices of altering the turnround performance of conventional cargo liners, of which (especially in the British-registered fleet) so many have been built in recent years. It has not compared the actual or potential performance of such ships with alternative techniques—such as those involving pallets, containers and roll-on, roll-off—on which many papers have been published in recent years. Some remarkable results have been reported—e.g. the simultaneous achievement of an 80 % improvement in turnround time (from 5 days to 1) and a 90 % reduction in stevedoring man-hours by changing from conventional to all-container operations. But such a change requires the purchase of many hundreds of containers (at £500 to £800 each) and the construction of specialized ships which, in general, cannot carry any substantial quantity of cargo not in containers (because the quayside movement of containers is parallel to the ship's fore-and-aft line and that of conventional break-bulk cargo at right angles to it). Such remarkable results can, in other words, be achieved only as a result of large capital expenditures, and then only in respect of a (possibly large) part of the total cargo moving in cargo liners.

It may, therefore, be suggested that comparisons between container operations (or other advanced cargo-handling techniques) and conventional cargo liners should not assume a continuation of past or present performance of the latter. This, however, is not to suggest that container, pallet and roll-on, roll-off techniques are uneconomic, or that they have not an important place in sea transport: merely that the great advantages they offer should be compared with the performance of conventional ships and techniques *after* any likely improvements in the latter have taken place.

7

TOWARDS AN ECONOMIC APPRAISAL
OF PORT INVESTMENTS[1]

There is widespread agreement[2] that port facilities in many countries
need improvement, partly to serve increased volumes of trade and
partly because it appears that substantial economies in the cost of sea
transport can only be achieved by improvements in seaports. The
object of this paper is to discuss methods by which such proposals
may be appraised. The discussion is, however, confined to proposals
to improve the point of contact between ship and port, rather than the
warehousing, processing, and other activities which also take place in
or near ports.

The scope of modern port investments

Rather more than 75 % of the aggregate tonnage of seaborne cargo
consists of oil or dry bulk cargoes (such as grain, ore, coal, sugar and
fertilisers of various kinds), and these are carried in ships in which
increased size can provide marked economies. As the size of ships
increases, so their capital, crew, fuel, insurance and maintenance
costs per ton of cargo diminish. Other costs, such as the dues levied
by port authorities, either fall to a smaller extent or remain the same.
For smaller ships the curves relating average cost per ton of cargo
carried to ship size fall steeply: for larger ones they fall much less.
The shorter the route length the smaller the ship size at which the

[1] I am indebted to Professor M. E. Beesley, Mr D. L. Munby, Mr R. Turvey,
Mr K. F. Glover and Mr P. Sinclare of the National Ports Council, and colleagues in the Board of Trade, the Ministry of Transport and HM Treasury, for
their encouragement and for commenting on several earlier versions of this
paper. None of these has any responsibility for any remaining errors and omissions. The views expressed are my own.
[1] e.g. at the 1964 UN Conference on Trade and Development. Its *Common
measure of understanding on shipping questions* stated, *inter alia*: 'All countries
should... give priority to improvement of port operations and connected inland
transportation facilities.' *UNCTAD Final Act*, Cmnd. 2417, HMSO 1964,
Annex A.Vi.22, page 421.

curves begin to flatten out.[1] There are therefore many projects, especially on the longer trade routes, for deepening existing ports to accommodate larger ships or for extending jetties or pipelines to deep water. Deepening an existing port is not confined to dredging the approach channels and docks, for bigger ships need deeper berths. Dredging alongside an existing quay may undermine the foundations and bring it down. The quay may, therefore, need to be completely reconstructed at a cost of, say, £1,000 per foot of quay face. Where the tidal range is large it may be necessary to reconstruct lock entrances as well as the quays, in order to increase the limiting lengths and breadths as well as the limiting depths of water.

Something less than 25 % of the tonnage of seaborne cargo consists of cargoes carried in cargo liners. Because of the need for frequent sailings scheduled in advance, special stowage and more careful handling, e.g. of manufactures, the cost of sea transport in cargo liners is very much higher than the cost of those commodities which can be pumped, poured or tipped into ships and sucked or grabbed out again. The aggregate of services rendered by cargo liners may well be as great as that of the ships carrying the other 75 % of world seaborne tonnage. The largest single reason for this is the cost of loading and discharging the ships, comprising first the port turn-round time and secondly the cash costs (mainly labour) of physically handling the cargo. The current proportion of time spent in port by cargo liners appears to be about 60 %, and in an earlier paper it has been argued[2] that if this could be reduced to 20 % the cost of sea transport in a cargo liner could be reduced by between 18 and 35 %, depending on the route length. The cash cost of handling the cargo ranges from about 20 to over 30 %. Both turnround time and handling costs can be substantially reduced by investment in modern berths with mechanical handling equipment and with transit sheds in which the floors are (*a*) level with the quay and the loading apron from land transport, and (*b*) sufficiently free from pillars to allow free movement for fork-lifts, tow-motors and trolleys. Moreover, these modern

---

[1] Cf. H. Benford, *et al.*: 'Current trends in the design of iron ore ships', *Trans. Soc. Nav. Archit. Mar. Engrs*, (New York, 1962), and *International Marine Design and Equipment* (Tothill Press, London, 1963).

[2] R. O. Goss: 'The turnround of cargo liners and its effect on sea transport costs', reprinted above, pp. 132–151.

berths will also have greatly increased annual capacities; although individual berths may be more expensive, therefore, fewer of them will be needed for any given flow of cargo.

The third principal method of reducing the costs of sea transport is to introduce radically new techniques. One of these is 'roll-on, roll-off'. In this goods remain on their land vehicles (rail or road, but usually the latter), which are then driven or towed over a ramp and through bow, stern or side doors into the ship and on to any of several decks. Another new technique is unitization, or the assembly of packages, etc., which were formerly stowed loose, into pallets, stillages or cribs capable of being handled mechanically, e.g. by fork-lifts. Some writers have maintained that palletization is the most economic form of unitization;[1] it has the advantage that the fairly small units (between 1 and 2 tons maximum, and frequently less) are more nearly the size of the typical liner consignment and therefore more appropriate for door-to-door movements. Both 'roll-on, roll-off' and unitization require substantial investment in port facilities such as ramps and parking and assembly areas, in pallets etc., and in mechanical handling equipment. Both will reduce ships' turnround time very considerably.

Unitization is seen at its most elaborate in the container concept. Containers[2] are rectangular boxes usually built to the specification[3] of the International Standards Organization (8 ft high, 8 ft wide, 10 or a multiple of 10 ft long, capable of being stacked and with corner castings designed to mate with special lifting, levelling and securing devices). Specialized gantry cranes (at about £250,000 apiece) are needed to lift them on and off the ships and the land vehicles which move them between the quay and the adjacent container park.

[1] For an extensive discussion of this question see *Norw. Ship. News*, 25 Jan. 1967, pages 50–9 (paper by T. Winsvold and subsequent discussion).
[2] An extensive literature on containers and containerization includes: R. T. Crake: 'Long distance container economics', *ICHCA Qly. Jour.*, Jan. 1963; D.T. Mallett: 'The container ship', *ICHCA Qly. Jour.*, Sept. 1955; J. MacN. Sidey: 'The commercial operation of containers', *ICHCA Qly. Jour.*, Jan. 1963; L. A. Harlander: 'Engineering development of a container system for the west coast-Hawaiian trade', *Trans. SNAME* (*Trans. Soc. Nav. Archit. Mar. Engrs, N.Y.*), Vol. 68, 1960; and 'Further developments of a container system for the west coast-Hawaiian trade', *Trans. SNAME*, Vol. 69, 1961.
[3] ISO Draft Recommendation 804 of 1965 and British Standard 3951 cover these and other sizes.

It is technically possible to stow a limited number of containers in conventional ships, but in order to obtain the cheap and rapid handling which is their justification they are best carried in ships designed specifically to carry them.[1] These have very wide hatches and vertical guides to assist in placing the containers precisely in position, and are capable of carrying them stacked on deck as well. Container ships are capable of loading and discharging both very rapidly and very cheaply. Thus, not only is it possible to achieve substantial reductions, in favourable circumstances, in the cost of sea transport (after allowing for the costs of the containers and other equipment), but transhipment in smaller vessels seems likely to become as common as it was in the days of cheap dock labour. These smaller ships will, however, be equally specialized. Their use will enable the deep-sea container ships to concentrate upon main ports only, instead of making a 'milk-round' of major and minor ports; thus all parts of the system will be able to operate at higher average load factors. Overall, the container concept appears to be capable, on suitable routes, of effecting as remarkable a revolution in sea transport as the substitution of steam for sail or of iron and steel ships for wooden ones. This effect is further assisted by the fact that, as optimal ship size varies directly with the speed of cargo-handling,[2] container ships can reap many of the economies of ship size which have hitherto been limited to tankers and dry bulk carriers. But these advantages again require substantial investment in port facilities: specialized berths, gantry cranes, and some 20 acres of hard standing per berth to act as a container park. Unitization, and particularly containerization, seems likely to have marked effects on proposals to expand port capacity to deal with any expected growth in trade, for the annual throughput capacity of a container berth appears to be roughly ten times that of an ordinary berth serving conventional cargo liners,[3] and it could well be more. But because specialized container ships have a very large annual

[1] The design and nature of container ships is summarized and described with numerous examples in: J. J. Henry and H. J. Karsch: 'Container ships', paper presented to SNAME (New York, Nov. 1966). See also R. J. Scott: 'Container-ship design', SNAME paper presented 26 Jan. 1962 to Great Lakes and Rivers Section, and D. A. Argyriadis, 'Cargo container ships', *Trans. R.I.N.A.*, 1959.
[2] See T. Thorburn: *Supply and demand for water transport* (Stockholm, 1960).
[3] Cf. *Portbury; Reasons for the Minister's decision not to authorise the construction of a new dock at Portbury, Bristol* (HMSO, 1966), page 10.

carrying capacity they are likely to be used only on the more heavily travelled routes; moreover, their advantages over conventional ships diminish as route length increases.[1]

The problem

Proposals to deepen ports, to reconstruct berths for the accelerated turnround of cargo liners, or to permit the use of roll-on, roll-off or unitization techniques all rank as important investment projects, often involving many millions of pounds. But there is no commonly accepted method of appraising proposals for investment in port facilities (i.e. of deciding *whether, how, when* and *where* any given proposal should be carried out). It is, for example, one thing to suggest that a port should be deepened to take larger ships: it is quite another to say that the optimal depth for either existing or proposed new works is *x* feet rather than some other figure, or that £*x* million should be spent on new facilities and that work should commence next year. Yet that is precisely the sort of decision that must be taken, somehow and by someone. In some instances this lack of systematic appraisal techniques appears to have led to under-investment, over-investment or misplaced and mistimed investment.[2] At least until recently, the situation may have been adequately described by Thorburn:[3] 'Large investments in harbours throughout the world appear to be made to a large extent intuitively and not on the basis of rational economic calculations.' In fact, many of them have been made as a result of representations from interested parties, and stem from vague and unquantified considerations of 'public need' rather than from any explicit calculations of economic advantages. This, no doubt, is largely due to the difficulties involved in estimating the net advantages of any given proposal, or the economic difference between the situa-

[1] Cf. Crake, *op. cit.* However, Crake's calculations are in many respects misleading, and his limit of 3,000 n.m. for efficient containership operation is certainly a serious understatement, quite apart from being a generalization not necessarily applicable to all routes.

[2] For the UK see the *Report of the Committee of Inquiry into the major ports of Great Britain (Rochdale Report)*, Cmnd. 1824 (HMSO, 1962), and the National Ports Council's: *Port development: an interim plan*, 1965.

[3] *Op. cit.*, page 140. See also *Rochdale Report*, e.g. para. 47, and E. F. Renshaw: 'A note on the measurement of the benefit from public investment in navigation projects', *American Economic Review*, Sept. 1957.

tion which would exist with the investment and that which would exist without it; it may also be associated with the fact that, until recent years, very few port authorities have employed economists. (Nor have academic or practising economists taken much interest in the subject.)[1]

Port authorities are generally public and have a remarkable diversity of powers, practices and forms.[2] Their revenue is obtained partly from letting or leasing land, buildings and equipment to shipowners, traders and other firms operating within the port area, and partly from rendering services on a commercial basis (as, for example, in Manchester, where the Manchester Ship Canal Company Ltd undertakes all quayside services); but the principal sources of revenue for most port authorities are the dues charged on ships and cargoes. These dues are payable respectively by shipowners and (normally) by the owners of the cargo.

These dues show remarkable diversity of form and amount. Even within a single port the tariff is often extremely complex: charges on ships may vary according to whether or not they enter enclosed docks and according to where they have come from, and charges on cargoes according to the commodities involved.[3] But the commonest form of charging for ships is a fixed scale per gross or net registered

---

[1] A notable exception is P. C. Omtvedt: *On the profitability of port investments*, Oslo, 1962, duplicated. But this is largely an elaborate exercise in queueing theory and is concerned with minimizing costs rather than maximizing either the profits of the port authority or the net social benefits of the project (cf. page 9). Queueing theory has indeed a significant part to play in this field, but not a leading role. See also R. T. Eddison and D. G. Owen: 'Discharging iron ore', *Operational Research Quarterly*, Sept. 1953; D. T. Steer and A. C. C. Page: 'Feasibility and financial studies of a port installation', *O.R. Qly.*, Sept. 1961; and R. Chapman and R. R. P. Jackson: *Operational research studies of port operation*, unpublished paper available from British Iron and Steel Research Association, 1963—to all of which the foregoing remarks also apply. Because all these are based on capital *charges* (e.g. depreciation and interest) instead of capital *costs*, they neglect the timing of capital expenditure. None of them employs discounting procedures.

[2] For UK see Dr James Bird: *The major seaports of the UK* (London, 1963), and *Rochdale Report*. Most authorities produce tariffs and annual reports: so does the British Transport Docks Board.

[3] A useful summary of port charges throughout the world is available in Capt. F. S. Campbell (ed.): *Port dues, charges and accommodation*, London, annual. The ports of London and Liverpool have recently very much simplified their cargo tariffs.

ton[1] covering a stated (and often quite lengthy) stay in the port. The dues on cargo usually take the form of charges per ton weight, but are sometimes quoted per standard barrel, case, bale, etc., and occasionally *ad valorem*. In some countries these charges for ships and cargo are termed 'side wharfage' and 'top wharfage' respectively.

This system of charging bears no necessary relationship to either the average or the marginal costs (short or long period) involved, and effectively prevents the use of discounted cash flow[2] techniques in the analysis of port investment projects (except buildings and equipment for rent or leasing and provision of direct services like cranage and cargo-handling). If a proposal to deepen a port is considered it will enable larger ships to be used at, very likely, lower costs. But, unless there is a significant diversion of cargo from other ports or a significant generation of cargo from lower freight rates, there will be fewer of the larger ships and roughly the same (gross or net) tonnage of shipping using the port in any given period as there would have been if the deepening had not taken place. At any given level of charges, therefore, the port authority's revenue from charges on both ships and cargo may be unchanged.[3]

---

[1] A gross ton is 100 cu.ft. of permanently enclosed space in the ship, leaving out 'exempted spaces' like double-bottom and peak tanks. Net tonnage is obtained from gross tonnage by the exclusion of 'deducted spaces' reckoned not to earn revenue, such as engine-room, crew, navigation and store spaces. But some of these deductions are made, not at their measured value, but after formulae have been applied. Neither gross nor net tonnage, therefore, has any necessary connection with either the volume or the weight of cargo that a ship is capable of carrying—still less with the cargo actually being carried on the relevant voyage. To make matters worse, a type of ship known as an 'open shelter-decker' has a large part of its cargo-carrying space exempt from all tonnage measurement. There are also variations between national tonnage measurement rules.

[2] Discounted cash flow techniques have been described in many recent works, of which the best-known are perhaps A. J. Merrett and Allen Sykes: *The finance and analysis of capital projects*, London, 1963, and NEDO: *Investment appraisal* (HMSO, 1965). For d.c.f. as applied to shipping see: 'Economic criteria for optimal ship designs', reprinted above, pp. 61–99 and 'The Economics of Automation in British Shipping', reprinted above, pp. 100–131.

[3] Cf. Maritime Transport Committee, OEEC, *Annual Report* 1963, paras. 102 and 103. The point is also implied in the White Paper: *Iron ore imports into South Wales*, Cmnd. 2706 (HMSO, 1965), paras. 3–5 and 17, although the discounted cash flow exercise referred to was in fact a discounted cost one. This was legitimate enough in the circumstances, since it could be reasonably assumed that the gross benefits were the same for each project. The arguments in this paper were also, to some extent, implicit in various papers delivered by the late

Again, given that port dues are levied on a fixed scale and for fixed periods, it follows that, if it is decided to construct (or to reconstruct) sheds or quays or to install new cargo-handling equipment so as to improve ships' turnround times, the port authority may still receive the same revenue as before. If the periods for which which ship dues are levied are short, so that after the investment is completed some ships become liable for fewer such periods, the port authority's revenue may even be reduced. Yet, as in the former example, the investment may well be producing net benefits to the trading community and ultimately to industrial consumers.

It is, of course, probable that if investment in port facilities leads to the cost of sea transport to and from that port being lower than it otherwise would have been, and if (as is very likely) this cost reduction is passed on to the consumers in the form of lower freight rates, there will be cargo generated and diverted from other ports. But there is no reason to suppose that this will produce sufficient revenue on the existing system of charges to make the results of discounted cash flow calculations socially optimal. This is even less likely where an improvement in port facilities can be expected to lead to changes in ships' load factors as well as in their sizes and speeds.

It cannot be argued that the answer to this problem is to raise port charges all round, for it is highly probable that some (possibly most) of the ships using the port will have obtained no benefit at all. They may be trading on short routes where the optimal ship size had been reached before any deepening took place; their size may be limited by the facilities in other ports or by canals; or they may be using quays and equipment which have not been improved. Nor can it necessarily be argued that a sliding scale of tonnage dues should be introduced so

Professor Sir John Biles, of which the latest was 'The draught and dimensions of the most economical ship', *Trans. Inst. Naval Architects* 1931, and in his *Memorandum on the economic size and speed of steam vessels* to the Dominions Royal Commission, 1914–17, Cd. 8460, 1917. See also *Depths to be provided in seaports, entrance channels and berths*, Permanent International Assoc. of Navigation Congresses, 1955, and L. Saville: 'Increase in cost of harbour and dock schemes due to increase in draught of ships', *Report No. 32, XIIIth International Congress of Navigation,* London, 1923, for estimates of the remarkable sensitivity of the capital cost of harbour works to small variations in the specified depths of water. A common suggestion is that the cost varies as the cube of the depth obtained. It is, however, obvious that the power depends, *inter alia,* upon the under-water angle of repose of the material concerned.

as to discriminate between ships according to the extent to which they use the new facilities. In any large port with a more or less continuous stream of related investment projects, this might introduce a quite unworkable complexity into the charging system. Further, the use of some of these facilities involves no social costs at all, and their socially optimal price is therefore zero. An example of this last point may be seen in the use of an uncongested dredged approach channel: no matter what the ship's size, the costs to the community are exactly the same whether the ship uses the channel or not; therefore, as in the classic question of tolls on bridges, the socially optimal answer is that when the channel is not congested the charge should be zero and that when it is congested the charge for any given ship should be equal to the increase in congestion costs that the ship imposes on all the other ships using the channel.[1] Moreover, as (for any given volume of cargo) larger ships means fewer ships, the deepening of a port may mean a reduction in congestion costs; if it were not that, first, large ships are less manoeuvrable than smaller ones, and secondly, the capital cost of harbour works varies as something like the cube of the depth of water,[2] it might be that large ships should be encouraged by the pricing system rather than otherwise.

The problem of the appraisal of investments by port authorities is, therefore, intimately related to the problem of charging for the services that they provide. The present system does not equate the charges actually levied with the social costs[3] of either ship or cargo,

---

[1] Cf. *Road pricing: the economic and technical possibilities* (HMSO, 1964), and various works cited therein. In the USA much dredging and waterway improvement is carried out by the US Army Corps of Engineers and financed by a combination of Federal and local government sources. Substantially, therefore, American port authorities do not charge dues for these 'conservancy' functions; e.g. the Port of New York Authority levies no port dues on this account. Neither, however, does it levy any equivalent of congestion costs. But see Renshaw, *op. cit.* (p. 156) and below (footnote, p. 162).

[2] See Saville, *op. cit.*, 1923, and PIANC, *op. cit.*, 1955 (footnote, p. 159).

[3] Given a rational pricing system for ports, there are few significant differences between private and social costs in this field. It is true that the first prosecution for smoke emission in the City of London was of a ship moored in the Upper Pool; it is also true that pollution of seas and beaches by oil and oily water discharged overboard can be a serious problem; but both are best dealt with by prohibition. This leaves, as the only significant externality, the congestion costs imposed by a ship on other ships in port approaches and in narrow seas like the Straits of Gibraltar and Dover. It seems that the nautical equivalent of traffic

and tonnage and cargo dues take little or no account of differences in costs to either the shipowner or the port authority. The existing system may possibly be of some use in the appraisal of investments designed to handle increases in the physical volume of trade but only with given techniques throughout. It is certainly not suitable for those involving the adoption of new techniques, whether of cargo-handling or ship size. In fact, it does not seem to have been developed either in order to allocate existing physical resources properly or in order to act as an investment indicator: its aim has been merely to raise sufficient revenue to cover 'costs', including explicit interest and depreciation. Until the Rochdale Report recommended that depreciation be based on a replacement instead of on a historic cost basis, this was a serious understatement of the social costs involved.

The overall social cost-benefit approach

Discounted cash flow involves taking account of the revenues and the cash costs over the life of the project (hence the term 'cash flow'), discounting them to a base year and subtracting the capital cost of the project (also discounted, if construction extends over more than one year). The result is termed net present value (NPV)—see Appendix, Part I, page 183. The discounted cash flow approach, in other words, takes account only of the advantages of the project to the investor; maximizing NPV will (except where the lives of mutually exclusive projects differ) lead to the optimal result for the investor. It will lead to a socially optimal result only if the pricing systems employed for inputs and outputs (and also for competing inputs and outputs) fully reflect the social costs involved, and not always even then. (The use of d.c.f. with socially optimal pricing would lead to very few bridges being built.)[1]

control may shortly be applied in the worst such places, as, indeed, it has been for some years amongst the larger transatlantic liners. The 'Torrey Canyon' disaster will encourage this.

[1] See C. D. Foster: *The transport problem*, Blackie, 1963, for an extensive discussion on this problem. It was first dealt with in two papers by Jules Dupuit: 'On the utility of public works' and 'On tolls and transport charges', *Annales des ponts et des chausées*, 1844 and 1849, translated and reprinted in *International Economic Papers*, Nos. 2 and 11 respectively.

Where d.c.f. is not a satisfactory method of investment appraisal, social cost-benefit analysis may be employed.[1] This means that, in addition to the cash flows, if any, the calculations take account of all the changes in social benefits and social costs which would result from the project, reducing them to monetary terms and discounting them to a present value from which the capital cost (or *its* present value if construction extends over more than one year) may be subtracted in order to obtain the net present value. The investment rules are the same as for d.c.f.: accept all projects with positive net present values; where they are mutually exclusive accept that which has the greatest NPV; and, where they are mutually exclusive in the sense of having alternative starting dates, select that starting date which provides the greatest NPV to the same base year. Except under capital rationing, cost-benefit ratios serve no useful purpose that NPV does not and have considerable disadvantages of their own, especially in respect of mutually exclusive projects.

The difficulties of cost-benefit analysis in this field do not lie so much in measuring the costs involved as in measuring the benefits. It might be thought that all that was needed was the consideration of differences in the market prices of sea transport services between the situation which exists with the investment and that which might

---

[1] There is an extensive and increasing literature on this subject, much of it recent. P. D. Henderson: 'Notes on public investment criteria in the United Kingdom', *Oxford Bulletin of Statistics*, Jan. 1965; A. R. Prest and R. Turvey: "Cost-Benefit Analysis: A Survey", *Economic Journal* Dec, 1965 and M. S. Feldstein: 'Cost-benefit analysis and investment in the public sector', *Public Administration*, Winter, 1964, survey the subject in general and cite numerous references. Published applications of cost-benefit analysis in the UK include: T. Coburn, M. E. Beesley and D. J. Reynolds: *The London–Birmingham motorway traffic: and economics*, HMSO, 1960; C. D. Foster and M. E. Beesley: 'Estimating the social benefit of constructing an underground railway in London', *Jl R. Statist. Soc.* 1963, and 'The Victoria line: social benefits and finance', *Jl R. Statist. Soc.* 1965; and various publications of the Road Research Laboratory. The US Army Corps of Engineers have attempted cost-benefit analysis of navigation projects; for a scathing critique of their methods see Renshaw, *op. cit.*, p. 156; but Renshaw omitted to criticize them for using cost-benefit ratios instead of net present values. See also *Feasibility studies, Economic and technical soundness analysis, Capital projects* and *Benefit cost evaluations as applied to aid financed water or related land-use projects* (Supplement No. 1 to preceding reference), USA Dept. of State, Agency for International Development, Office of Engineering, Washington, DC. Both still propose the use of cost-benefit ratios and neither gives any very clear indication of how economies in ship costs are to be included.

reasonably be expected to exist without it. But the pricing of sea transport is itself no simple matter. For tramp ships, dry bulk carriers and tankers, which carry mainly near-homogeneous commodities, usually on charter-parties of one sort or another, the 'price' of sea transport may be quoted per ton of cargo or, very often, as a rate of hire for the ship, daily or per ton deadweight per month. Most charter-parties, especially time-charters, leave some costs to be paid by the charterer in addition to the payments made to the shipowner; i.e. they do not represent the total cost of sea transport.[1] These rates fluctuate from day to day, often markedly, both absolutely and, for different cargoes, routes, types and sizes of ships, relatively to one another. Such fluctuations, which depend essentially on the world supply-demand position for the different sorts of shipping, are very difficult to predict except in the broadest terms—or, very often, at all. Moreover, for obvious reasons, it is difficult to observe different rates for ships of different sizes carrying the same commodities over the same route at the same time.

For cargo liners, which carry heterogeneous cargoes and have more stable and simpler rates agreed in shipping conferences (their rates are usually quay to quay—i.e. including the cost of loading and discharging the ship), the same rates are usually applied regardless of the type, size and speed of ship;[2] but different rates are applied to different commodities. In many trades the tariffs are not published and, even if they were, it would not be possible to calculate average rates of freight, partly because most published statistics of international trade do not distinguish between goods carried in liners and those carried in other ships, partly because the tariff and statistical commodity classifications are different and partly because these are often based on different measures of cargo, such as numbers, value, or tons weight (for trade statistics) and tons weight, tons measurement (this time of

[1] See J. Bes: *Chartering and shipping terms*, 2nd ed., C. de Boer (Amsterdam, 1951); and H. Gripaios: *Tramp shipping* (Nelson, London, 1959).

[2] For a general description of pricing in shipping conferences see D. Marx, Jr: *International shipping cartels* (Princeton, 1953); W. L. Grossman: *Ocean freight rates* (Cornell, 1956); D. L. McLachlan *Pricing in ocean transportation* (unpublished Ph.D. thesis), (Leeds, 1959), and 'The price policy of shipping conferences', *Scott. Jour. Pol. Econ.*, 1963; and R. O. Goss: 'The regulation of sea transport', reprinted above, pp. 13–24 and works cited therein.

40 cu.ft.) or tons weight *or* measurement at shipowners' option (for the tariffs).

In neither tramp nor cargo-liner trades, therefore, is it possible to employ observed market prices. Nor, since the whole point of a port investment may be to permit the use of a different (e.g. larger) type of ship, is it possible to confine the effects to economies in operating costs. Economies in capital cost are just as relevant. Thus the method proposed in this paper is fundamentally different from that usually employed, e.g. in road studies, where it can legitimately be assumed that after construction or improvement the road will be used by much the same sort of vehicles as before. It is necessary to approach the problem in a different way.

If, for any given type and size of ship operating under any given conditions (e.g. of cargo and route), we can estimate the initial and operating costs (ideally this should include the distribution over the life of the ship of operating costs and of periods when it is out of service for the periodic surveys required by classification societies), we can perform a discounted cash flow calculation, discounting at the opportunity cost of capital,[1] with various assumed average rates of freight per ton of cargo. Each will, of course, produce a different NPV. One such freight rate will produce an NPV of zero—i.e. the internal rate of return[2] will be equal to the opportunity cost of capital. At any freight rate higher than this, shipping will provide more profitable investments than could reasonably be expected elsewhere. It may be assumed that shipowners will then order more ships and that competition will force both the freight rate and the internal rate of return downwards. Conversely, at any lower freight rate shipowners will be less willing to invest in ships, the supply of ships will be reduced and both the freight rate and the internal rate of return on ships will rise. The freight rate which provides an internal rate of return equal to the opportunity cost of capital is therefore the long-term equilibrium rate for the assumed shipping techniques.

[1] For the UK this is generally taken to be in the range of 6 to 8 %. See Merrett and Sykes: *op. cit.*; A. M. Alfred: *Discounted cash flow and corporate planning*, Woolwich Economic Papers, No. 3; and NEDO: *op. cit.* (p. 158).

[2] The internal rate of return is obtained by the solution of a d.c.f. equation for *r* at zero NPV; this may be directly compared with the (opportunity) cost of capital. See Appendix, Part I.

This concept, which is really no more than a refined version of average total cost, is generally referred to as a 'shadow price',[1] it is better thus described than as 'average total cost' because it is not, in any ordinary sense of the word, an average. The usual definition of average total cost assumes that output and cost levels are capable of being maintained (in real terms) over the life of the capital assets concerned; a shadow price can take account of any variations over the life of the ship in either costs (e.g. repair costs) or output levels (e.g. from periods out of service for quadrennial surveys and repair). The formal definition of the shadow price for the purpose of this paper is 'that level of price at which the discounted revenue, on the specified level and pattern of outputs, exceeds the discounted cash operating costs for the same level and pattern of outputs by the capital cost involved *minus* the discounted scrap value, if any'. It may, of course, take account of the savings in packing and pilferage costs claimed for containerization.

There is, however, no necessary relationship between the shadow price and the level of freight rates at any particular time. The former reflects long-term costs; the latter reflects both the highly variable supply-demand position of world shipping and also the considerable opportunities which currently exist, e.g. by way of cheap export credit, for shipowners to obtain capital at less than its private opportunity cost. It is obvious that such rates of interest are irrelevant for the purposes of this paper. Given the long life of most ships (from 12 to 20 years for tankers to 25 to 35 years for passenger liners), the inelastic short-run supply and the inelastic short-run demand, market freight rates will often be very different from shadow price levels. High or low market rates, however, will not necessarily affect the differences in net social benefits between ships operating, as a result of investment in ports, at improved levels of efficiency; and it is the differences in shadow prices associated with these improvements in efficiency which can be used to estimate the benefits from investments in ports. The different levels of efficiency may include those due to

---

[1] See, e.g. R. Dorfman, P. A. Samuelson and R. M. Solow: *Linear programming and economic analysis* (McGraw-Hill, 1958). S. G. Sturmey: *On the pricing of tramp ship services* (Institute of Shipping Research, Bergen, 1965), and University of Lancaster Department of Economics Occasional Paper No. 4, refers to this as the 'continuation rate'.

changes in ship size, type, speed or any other physical alteration in the ships themselves, to alterations in operating conditions, such as turnround and load factor, and to any (specified) combination of these. The difference between the shadow price in the conditions which would exist without the investment and the shadow price in the conditions which are estimated to exist with the investment is a preliminary measure of the change in social costs per ton of cargo. Some other costs and benefits are dealt with later in this paper.

In estimating the change in shadow prices it is important to allow for any probable changes in the quantity of cargo moving; otherwise the change in shadow prices will be based solely on changes in supply conditions and will fail to take account of the elasticity of demand. The allowances for diverted and generated cargo are also discussed later.

It must be admitted that this technique of using shadow prices has at least five disadvantages. First, it does not allow for differences in uncertainty between shipping and industry generally, and it is from the latter that estimates of the opportunity cost of capital must be derived. Shipping is a peculiarly uncertain industry in which to invest because it is subject to booms and slumps which are sometimes independent of fluctuations in world trade (the severe shipping slump of 1957 took place as a result of over-building and over-ordering of ships in the preceding boom years, and in spite of a fairly steady increase in the tonnage of seaborne trade throughout the slump years). But, as we are proposing to use differences in shadow prices rather than their absolute levels, this should not matter much unless the ships which use the new port facility are more capital-intensive than they otherwise would have been. Sometimes, especially in the context of deepening or unitization proposals, this may be so; moreover ships, especially large ones, are more capital-intensive than industry generally (replacement cost per man ranges up to £40,000 for a cargo liner and up to £150,000 for a 140,000-ton deadweight tanker). It follows that it may be desirable to raise the rate of discount for ships by a percentage point or so. In general, the practice of allowing for uncertainty by raising the discount rate is to be deplored, because it is more accurate and useful to estimate the spread of uncertainty in the specific components concerned and thus to produce 'upper', 'lower' and 'probable' estimates of NPV. But in this con-text the item subject to the greatest uncertainty is the freight rate, and this is not an input to our calculation at all: it is the output. Thus there appears to be no other way of including uncertainty in calcula-tions of this nature. On the other hand it is entirely possible that ship-owners and long-term time-charterers will have learnt that over-optimism in shipping leads to slumps and will not react to future periods of high freights in such an exaggerated manner. Some parts of the shipping trade press currently lose no opportunity of making the point.

Secondly, the use of differences in shadow prices as calculated on a shipowner's view of net cash flows involves taking taxes, tax allow-ances and investment grants into account. The last two encourage more capital-intensive ship designs—i.e. ships that are larger, faster, more extensively equipped or technically more advanced. It could be argued that taxes and investment grants are merely transfer payments and should be ignored in any calculation of social benefits. But the effects of taxes, tax allowances and investment grants are intended; and, if it is public policy to encourage the building of larger, faster or more extensively equipped ships, it would be strange to ignore these effects when considering investments in an industry as closely related as that of ports. Whether their inclusion makes any significant dif-ference depends upon the levels and incidence of taxes, tax allowances and investment grants, upon the tax position of the individual ship-owner (i.e. whether he has sufficient profits to take full advantage of his tax allowances—this was recently relevant in the United Kingdom because of depressed profits in shipping and investment allowances, and it is still relevant because of depressed profits and free deprecia-tion). With the present British tax system as it applies to shipping, the present value of taxes and tax allowances taken together is generally about zero and the shadow price will therefore be un-affected by their inclusion or exclusion. Investment grants, however, do affect the shipowners' calculations, and do so markedly; therefore they should be included. But they produce both 'income' and 'substitution' effects; i.e. they make shipping more profitable than it would have been with given techniques but without the grants, and they also affect the optimal technique. This could be overcome by taking ships designed with investment grants in mind and calculating the shadow price without the investment grant. Thus the substitution effect would be included but not the income effect. However, since investment incentives are provided in order to reflect social benefits associated with an investment which do not accrue to the investor (e.g. by equalizing the private and social marginal efficiency of capital), the income effects should be included.

Thirdly, the costs of a conventional (i.e. non-unitized) cargo liner carrying heterogeneous cargoes will to some extent depend on the 'mix' of commodities carried, because different commodities have different cargo-handling costs, speeds and stowage factors.[1] A general reduction in (real) freight rates may, if the elasticity of demand for sea transport differs between commodities, alter the mix, the cargo-handling costs, the turnround times and, therefore, the shadow prices. But this is unlikely to matter very much. First, unitization of cargo is likely to grow and to reduce the spread of cargo-handling costs and speeds between different commodities; secondly, changes in the mix are more likely to come from other causes, such as the re-location of producing or consuming centres. If there is any substantial force in the point it is likely to be made obvious enough by market research. It is probable that the remainder may be neglected without substantial error.

Fourthly, it might be that, if the port investment being considered was very large in relation to the level of world trade being carried in ships of the type concerned, an actual surplus of such ships might result. It is conceivable that a large series of deepening projects, for example, might render some smaller dry bulk-carriers or tankers idle; again, a really massive improvement in the turnround of cargo liners or the widespread adoption of unitization might lead to a slump in dry-cargo shipping generally, i.e. to a marked increase in

---

[1] The stowage factor is the number of cu.ft. of cargo space occupied by one long ton: thus 2240 lbs of baled wool occupies 120 to 140 cu.ft., so baled wool has a stowage factor of 120 to 140; iron ore has a stowage factor of about 18. Stowage factors for many commodities are conveniently listed in R. E. Thomas: *Stowage: the properties and stowage of cargoes* (5th ed. rev. by O. O. Thomas), (Brown, Son & Ferguson, Glasgow, 1963), an indispensable compendium on cargo stowage.

laid-up tonnage.[1] But it is unlikely that port investments on such a scale could be carried out without lengthy warning to shipowners. Most port investments are technically elaborate and involve gestation periods of some years; given a ship life of 20 years, it follows that even in two years some 10 % of the world fleet would probably be scrapped. Moreover, the investment would need to be enormous to produce any such effect on world shipping—the construction of a major canal, such as the proposed sea-level canal at Panama, is the only likely project in such a scale.

Fifthly, the calculations ideally require the prediction of real costs and output levels in each year of the ship's life, and no data, not even historical data, exist on this subject. But it is possible to assume constancy; while this will raise all the shadow prices, it will not necessarily have any significant effect on the differences between them. Moreover, an assumption of constancy in costs and output levels greatly simplifies the calculations, and it is quite easy to allow for rising real wages in calculations of this type. For that matter, it is just as easy to allow for declining real insurance premiums. Both can be dealt with by reducing the time streams concerned to their (negative) present values and adding them to the capital cost.

In general, therefore, shadow prices as defined above can be used, possibly on the basis of a discount rate a percentage point or so higher than the opportunity cost of capital. But it would be quite wrong merely to multiply the difference in shadow prices by the tonnages of cargo estimated to flow, either without the investment or with it; either of these would imply a demand curve of a most improbable shape. The first would imply that there was neither diversion of cargo from other ports nor generation of cargo. The second would imply that the demand curve was horizontal at the level of the upper shadow price, turning in a right angle straight down at the level of the larger cargo tonnage.

This problem occurs in most cost-benefit analyses and can be overcome in the usual way. The cargo tonnage which would have existed in a given year without the investment may be multiplied by the full

[1] This appears to have happened in 1920, though not as a result of any planned series of port investments. See D. H. Aldcroft: 'Port congestion and the shipping boom of 1919–20', *Business History*, June 1961. There appears to be a distinct possibility that it may happen again as a result of containerization.

change in shadow prices and added to the product of the increase in cargo tonnage (i.e. the sum of diverted and generated tonnages) and half the change in shadow prices. (It may, however, be noted that, strictly speaking, the diversion and generation of cargo will depend on the change in *market* prices, and these, in long-term equilibrium, will reflect the income and substitution effects of both investment grants and cheap capital.) This allows for the slope of the demand curve and assumes that it is a straight line; if we had any evidence that it was any other shape we should use it. The procedure also assumes that diverted cargo comes from many competing ports or that it moves to many inland destinations or from many inland origins. Where a substantial proportion of diverted cargo moves to or from one inland point (e.g. if the port investment leads to the relocation of a plant dealing with a substantial proportion of diverted cargo), it may be necessary to deal with it separately. An example of this last point might be the construction at the mouth of an estuary of a new facility intended to divert cargo from up-river berths.

When we have thus obtained the change in consumers' surplus for any given year, it can be discounted to its present value and added to the present value (to the same base year) of the other years of the project's life. To produce the net present value, in social terms, of the project it merely remains (*a*) to add the change, if any, in the port authority's revenue from dues on cargo resulting from the project (it is assumed that dues on the ships have been included in the shadow price calculations and that dues on the cargo have been excluded), and (*b*) to subtract the associated change in the social costs (including capital and operating costs for the port authority and any changes in the need for working capital, e.g. to finance the larger stockpiles associated with larger ships, for traders) as and when they occur. Both items must be similarly discounted to their present value to the same base year. (See Appendix, Part II, pages 183–6). The value of new land created or reclaimed by pumping dredging spoil ashore, e.g. on to former marshland, may also be added as and when the land becomes available for use.

In other words, this method may be applied for any degree of improvement of existing works or for any level of investment in new facilities, and for any starting date that might produce an optimal answer. The investment rules enable one to choose the project giving the greatest net social benefit. Given that the improved port facilities are available to all shipowners on equal terms and that there is effective competition between them, this benefit will be passed on to the consumers. This is likely in practice since, even with the determination of freight rates by shipping conferences, the principal limitation on raising freight rates is the likelihood of attracting new competition; thus, if costs fall for the existing operators it will be obvious to all concerned that they have also fallen for any potential competitors.

National planning

It is obvious that port investments must be co-ordinated with whatever systems of national and regional planning may be in use in the nation concerned. This raises questions outside the scope of this paper; it also raises the question 'At which port shall we invest?' If mutually exclusive or competing investments at different ports produced by independent port authorities, each acting in (partial) ignorance of proposals being considered by the others and of the estimates being employed, were compared in terms of the method stated above, the absurd situation might be produced that investments at, say, the port of Alpha were being justified partly on the basis of cargo diverted from the ports of Beta and Gamma, while, simultaneously, investments at Beta and Gamma were justified partly by the inclusion of the same cargo plus diversions from Alpha. This could lead to serious over-investment. The procedure to avoid this trap is for a central authority to consider, first, the NPV of improving each port alone (i.e. assuming that the others are not improved) and including diverted cargoes and, secondly, the NPV of improving each possible combination, e.g. Alpha and Beta but not Gamma, or all three, and so on. In these instances there may be diversions of cargo in any or all directions or none; the diversions will almost certainly be different from those assumed in the first set of calculations. Obviously, this could give rise to a large number of calculations; but common sense will usually eliminate the less successful, and, as each will contain many components of the others (e.g. in respect of the 'basic' cargo flows and the shadow prices), there will be a far less than proportionate increase in calculation time for the remainder.

Except where the port investment is being appraised by an international body, as for example in the context of overseas aid (and possibly even then), there is also the question of the international division of the consumers' surpluses. Most governments seek to maximize the welfare of their own residents, not (apart from aid programmes) those of other nations; and where port authorities have user representatives they are usually drawn from their own nationals. It is, however, obvious that a reduction in transport costs between two countries may benefit one or the other or both. This raises questions in the economics of international trade which, at least in practical terms, are not easy to answer.[1] It may be noted that, in principle, the problem of the international division of benefits from investments appraised by cost-benefit analyses also arises in other fields, though since international trade is seldom directly involved, to a far smaller extent than with ports.[2] As C. B. Winsten has vividly remarked,[3] social benefits flow outwards from an investment like ripples on a pool and different results may be obtained by following the ripples to different distances.

The point may be clarified by stating the limiting cases. Where a purely entrepôt trade is concerned, i.e. where the producers, the processors and the consumers of the products are all situated outside the investing country, the *effective* consumer of sea transport (i.e. he who will benefit from a reduction in its market price) does not belong to that nation; none of the consumers' surplus will then remain within that territory and (from a national point of view) the port investment

[1] The problem is very similar to that dealt with in the theory of customs unions in that both involve the reduction of barriers to international trade. Port investments, however, cannot be assumed to be cost-free, and the international division of costs can be identified.

[2] The possibility does not seem to have attracted much attention from any of the authors cited, but it casts, nevertheless, a new light on the wording of the USA Flood Control Act of 22 June 1936: 'It is the sense of Congress that...the Federal Government should...participate in the improvement of navigable waters...if the benefits *to whomsoever they may accrue* are in excess of the estimated costs' (US Code, 1964, Vol. 8, Title 33, sect. 70(*a*), Italics added).

[3] Discussion on Foster and Beesley: *op. cit.* (1963), page 79.

may be appraised on a d.c.f. basis, regardless of whether the pricing system and level are socially optimal in the wider sense or not. Similarly, if the nation faces a completely inelastic demand curve for exports or a completely inelastic supply curve for imports, the effective consumer of sea transport is in the foreign country and the whole of the increase in consumers' surplus will be outside the investing country.

At the opposite extreme all the consumers' surplus will remain within the investing country if the trade is wholly within its territory, or if there is an infinitely elastic demand curve for exports or an infinitely elastic supply curve for imports. It may, however, be noted that either of these latter circumstances produces just as much reason, even from a purely national point of view, *and as far as investments designed to serve that single trade route are concerned,* for investing in the ports of the foreign country at the opposite end of the trade as in one's own ports. But the vast majority of port investments are designed to serve a large number of trade routes.

The proportion of consumers' surplus which remains within the investing country therefore varies, in respect of exports, directly as the elasticity of demand for the goods concerned and, in respect of imports, directly as the elasticity of supply. But these are unlikely to be susceptible to precise estimation over the life of a substantial investment in port facilities, particularly as the elasticities of both demand and supply may be expected to increase as trading habits, consumers' tastes, producers' disutilities and the technological situations of producers and consumers are adjusted to the new price levels. This last point, however, when combined with the lengthy gestation period of most port investments, suggests that the elasticities of supply and demand ought to be assumed to be fairly high—i.e. that most of the consumers' surplus will remain within the investing country. In that case, contrary to the initial reaction of most people working in this field, the volumes of generated and diverted cargo must be fairly large. Further refinement of this point will depend mainly upon the provision of more precise estimates of the elasticities involved in international trade, and especially the long-run elasticities. In the meantime, however heroic they may appear, assumptions cannot logically be avoided.

While the possibility that some of the change in consumers' surplus may accrue outside the investing nation tends to reduce the attractiveness of a project, there are benefits which, for the sake of clarity, have so far been mentioned only in passing. Faster turnround for cargo liners (especially when they spend only 40 % of their time at sea) does not mean merely that, because the ships can be used more intensively, the shadow price falls; it also means faster transit from origin to destination. Thus not only has the social cost of the service fallen, but the quality has risen too. In appropriate instances, allowance should be made for this.

The literature of transport economics is startlingly sparse on the subject of how to estimate the benefit to consumers from reductions in the transit time for goods.[1] Conceptually, four effects may be identified:

(a) Because the goods are at risk for a shorter time the insurance costs may be lower. But most of the risk to goods moving by sea comes in their handling, and neither this nor the sea passage will be significantly affected. It seems likely, therefore, that this point may be ignored.

(b) There is a reduced risk of market fluctuation while the goods are in transit. But this applies only to goods for which an urgent need arises suddenly, perhaps for technical reasons (e.g. spare parts for a ship's main engine) or because of changes in fashion. Such goods are more likely to travel by air than by sea, and this point, too, may well be too insignificant to warrant explicit calculation.

(c) Inventory control can be maintained more easily—i.e. smaller stocks are needed to maintain the same average lag between the receipt of an order and the delivery of the goods. In most instances this effect too is unlikely to be very large.

(d) Less working capital is needed for importers and exporters. This may be a significant factor. Let us consider a typical cargo liner on a round voyage of 10,000 miles. It is commonly accepted—there are no adequate statistics on the subject—that

---

[1] Coburn, Beesley and Reynolds: *op. cit.*, treated it as negligible. With a 40 minute saving between London and Birmingham this may well have been true but it is not so in the present context.

the current average of time spent in port is 60 %. If on that basis the shadow price per ton of cargo is £7·33 and if the time in port is reduced to the minimum credible proportion of 20 %, the shadow price becomes £5·36[1]. Thus there is a saving of £1·97 per ton of cargo. The (unweighted) average saving in transit time (from mid-loading to mid-discharge) is about $18\frac{1}{2}$ days, and if the cargo is valued at an average of £200 per ton the saving on working capital at 6 % is £0·608 per ton, or 30·9 % of the change in shadow prices. Even if all the other effects are dismissed as insignificant, this one is still sufficient to be taken into account. Some of this saving in working capital will itself accrue to people outside the country concerned.

This change in working capital consists largely of stockpiles or goods awaiting transit at the ports concerned; these should be capable of estimation. It should be noted that larger ships, operating less frequently, may lead to an increase in working capital and, possibly, also in storage facilities. This applies to tankers and dry bulk carriers, and may also (despite the reduction in *minimum* transport times) apply to container ships where annual capacities are so great that service frequencies may be reduced to maintain load factors.

One investment designed to permit the use of larger ships—the deepening of entrances in tidal waters—will have the additional effect of increasing the proportion of time during which the entrance can be used. Thus queueing effects will be reduced. Moreover, whether ships' arrival frequencies follow a random distribution or not, the provision of more berths may also reduce waiting time. See the sources cited on page 157 above.

Practical problems

There is no doubt that decisions on the optimal level and form of investment in ports have to be taken with reasonable facility. It may, with further research, be possible to refine many of the foregoing ideas, but if they cannot readily be quantified they will not be of very much use in the solution of the practical problems which arise in this field. There is therefore a need for a method, such as that suggested

---

[1] See R. O. Goss: *op. cit.* (pp. 132–151 above), for the shadow prices of a cargo operating on a wide variety of route lengths and cargo-handling speeds.

above, using components which can be estimated in practical terms and for which the calculation time and effort are not such that the start of physical work on an urgent project will be delayed in the interests of intellectual elegance.

The first step is obviously marketresearc h; if there is no great demand for the proposed facilities there is proportionately little case for providing them. It would be outside the scope of this paper to discuss market research at length. But it may be remarked that estimates of traffic flow commonly accompany current proposals for large-scale port investment projects, and the methods advocated in this paper do not, in principle, require any more information on this subject than is needed by any other method of appraisal save the division between the flow of cargo which would have existed without the investment and that which would exist with it (i.e. the diverted and generated flows). And, since any port authority's revenue calculations must similarly be based on a comparison of 'with' and 'without' situations, it follows that, if there is sufficient data to calculate the incremental revenue for a project on a given tariff structure, there is probably sufficient to indicate the incremental (i.e. the diverted and generated) cargo flows.

The second step is the calculation of shadow prices. For this, ships' capital and operating costs, load factors and (ideally) output levels over time are required. For iron ore carriers Professor Benford has published curves[1] which significantly resemble the concept of shadow prices described in this paper. These are curves of so-called 'required freight rate' or average total cost: as mentioned earlier, they show this falling steeply as a ship's deadweight tonnage increases at low levels, and gradually less steeply as it increases by equal increments to high levels. Professor Benford's calculations, however, appear to be open to the following criticisms:

(*a*) Although they are related to the factor prices and efficiencies of major unsubsidized maritime powers (i.e. not to those of the USA) and take a tax rate of 52 % into account, they do not allow for investment allowances or grants. The result is to overstate the cost of capital and, because large ships are more capital-intensive than small ones, to understate the relative

[1] (Footnote, page 153).

advantages of the large ship as well as to overstate the costs of all sizes of ships (i.e. to reduce the slope of the curves and to raise them).

(b) A 'capital recovery factor' (i.e. a ratio of profit before depreciation and after tax to initial cost, allegedly constant over the life of the ship—see (d) below) of 10 % is employed. Half of this is allowed for depreciation (a 20-year life being reasonable for this purpose); the remainder gives roughly 10 % on the mean of book values in the first and last years. If this were significantly higher than the opportunity cost of capital, then, because large ships are more capital-intensive than small ones, it would reduce the slope of the curves. But in fact a capital recovery factor of 10 % is equivalent to a discount rate very slightly in excess of 8 %, and this is, as noted earlier, the upper range of the credible values for the private opportunity cost of capital after tax and in real terms.

(c) The vessels chosen are of an unusual type, being powered by the steam turbines usually provided in USA-built ships. Elsewhere the more economical diesel engines are now used, though there is still some use of turbines for the larger powers. This probably raises all the curves and may affect their slopes as well. Moreover, Professor Benford has chosen a somewhat unusual combination of length, beam, maximum legal draft and operating draft.

(d) No allowance is made for the irregular incidence, throughout the ship's life, of repair costs and periods out of service. Because these occur simultaneously they necessarily have marked effects on the pattern of net cash flows, frequently to the extent of changing its sign; these effects are further exaggerated by the 1–2 year lag in the collection of taxes in some countries, including Denmark, France, Italy, the Netherlands, Spain, Sweden and the United Kingdom. These effects get stronger as the ship gets older and subject to more thorough surveys, so that, as noted earlier, the effect of ignoring these irregularities in net cash flows is to understate net present value and to overstate the 'required freight rates'. It probably does not affect the slope of the curves, though the absence of any published research on the varying (or possibly constant) incidence of survey costs and periods with varying ship size must leave us in some doubt on this point. As noted above, this approximation may be justifiable; it is certainly necessary for the time being.

Notwithstanding these criticisms of Professor Benford's work, it remains, for the time being, the best such study that we have. Until better calculations have been made we shall not know how big the errors are; it is entirely possible that for all practical purposes they are insignificant. Meanwhile, therefore, we should use his data in respect of projects intended to permit the use of larger bulk carriers.

In respect of cargo liners and conventional (i.e. general-purpose) tramp ships the earlier paper already cited should be of some use. In respect of roll-on, roll-off and unitized (including container) ships no fully adequate data has yet been published.

The proper discount rate for cost-benefit calculations has been the subject of lengthy academic controversy, and it is not proposed to enter into the discussion here. Most of the relevant arguments have been summarized in the papers by P. D. Henderson and by A. R. Prest and R. Turvey. With the results of the market research, the shadow prices and a rate of discount, present values can be calculated.

The financial implications

It may well be thought that, if investments in port facilities are to be appraised on a cost-benefit basis (i.e. on the assumption that the increased net revenue obtained by the port authority will not be sufficient to pay the capital charges), some form of subsidy will be required. Obviously many forms are possible: cheap capital[1] and outright subsidies are only two. But in fact this conclusion does not follow from the preceding arguments at all. It would be perfectly possible to appraise projects on a cost-benefit basis and, while construction was in progress, so to alter the charging system in use by port authorities that there would be an increase in the port authority's cash flow sufficient to defray the capital charges. This might well involve a drastic reconstruction of the whole charging system (except

---

[1] Many port authorities, however, can already obtain capital at, in effect, subsidized rates, so there is no necessary requirement for any special provisions. This is of some importance, since it follows that the proposals in this paper do not entail any weakening of the existing financial discipline.

for rents of land and buildings in the dock area and the charges for services rendered by the port authority). It might, for example, involve the substitution of berth-rents, payable in respect of very short periods of time, e.g. per day or per tide, plus lockage fees or other exit and entry fees as appropriate, all of which could (given sufficient research) be based upon marginal social costs. Since it is generally agreed that some parts of most ports are congested, it would follow that marginal social cost charging must give rise to positive charges in most instances; and where there are facilities which are not congested the imposition of reduced (or even zero) charges would encourage their use, thereby reducing the congestion elsewhere.

This immediately raises the question whether the marginal cost to be used is short or long-period marginal cost. It is generally assumed[1] that these two must be different, usually because it is thought that short-run marginal costs include only wages, material, fuel and the like, while long-run marginal costs include all these and capital charges too. But it has been shown[2] that, provided an optimal investment policy can be assumed to have been followed in the *recent* past, the average total cost for the output concerned will be on the long-run average total cost curve or envelope at a point where the short-run average total cost curve is tangential to it. It follows that short and long-period marginal costs must be equal; moreover, since the existence of congestion implies that the port is on the rising part of the long-run average total cost curve, it also follows that, at this point of equality, marginal costs must exceed average total costs. But there are often marked indivisibilities in port investments, and it is therefore unlikely that all competing ports could have followed an optimal investment policy throughout the whole of the recent past. Subject to this, congested ports priced on a marginal social cost basis should, therefore, be profitable; they also provide excellent opportunities for investment, and this investment will itself reduce social costs, e.g. of congestion, and therefore the charges. If it is clear that a port has not had an optimal investment policy in the recent past, then short and

---

[1] See, e.g. A. A. Walters: 'The long and short of transport', *Bull. Oxf. Univ. Inst. Statist.* May 1965.

[2] R. Turvey: 'Marginal Cost Pricing in Practice', *Economica*, Nov. 1964, a review article of a book of the same title edited by J. R. Nelson, 1964. The argument, however, depends on the cost functions being continuous.

long-period marginal costs will be different. A pricing policy based on short-run marginal social cost will then provide a good indication for most investment proposals. As far as the United Kingdom is concerned, it should be pointed out that any policy involving either marginal (social or private) cost pricing or significant profits would not be in accordance with the recommendations of the Rochdale Report. That report, however, discussed only the level of charges, rather than their structure, and did not mention either external costs and benefits or marginal cost pricing in any form.

Such a pricing policy would, of course, contrast strongly with the current system of charging gross (or net) tonnage dues on ships. If the cost of a new or improved berth varies as the cube (or even the square) of the depth, so may the charge. The gross and net tonnages of the ship, and therefore the total charge under the current system, also tend to vary roughly as the cube of the ship's draft (for similar types of ships). But the objections to the current system are: first, that it is only very loosely related to the length of time that the ship spends in port, and secondly that the charge is still calculated on the ship and not on the facilities it is using; it does not therefore promote the efficient use of berths of different qualities in the short term, nor does it give any economic indications of investment needs for the long term. It may be thought that such a reform of the pricing of port services is long overdue anyway, and for reasons not wholly dependent upon investment appraisal. It is currently under consideration in the United Kingdom under the auspices of the National Ports Council. Any basing of port pricing upon either short or long-term marginal costs is, however, bound to be difficult, partly because of the lack of research into the relevant cost functions and partly because of the discrete and variable nature of the unit of 'production' and the indivisibilities noted above.

Conclusion

If world trade is to expand at the rates suggested by all responsible authorities, investment in port facilities is needed. To some extent this can take the form of reconstruction and replacement of obsolete quays and warehouses so as to raise the productivity of the labour employed in loading and unloading the ships (which would be reflected both in ships' turnround times and in cargo handling costs); there is also a need for deep-water facilities for the handling of bulk commodities and for specialized berths for unit systems of cargo handling. In general there has in the past been serious under-investment and no generally accepted technique for appraising investment projects. This paper has attempted to outline methods which can be applied to the problems of whether to invest, how to invest, when to invest and where to invest.

Because of the non-optimal pricing technique employed by port authorities, optimal results cannot be produced by discounted cash flow methods. Cost-benefit analysis raises difficulties peculiar to this field, but it is suggested that they can be overcome by the use of calculated shadow prices as representing the social costs of sea transport and the application of techniques developed in other contexts. Because ports are, to some extent, alternatives to one another, because decision-making in this field is not an instantaneous process and because a port authority cannot reasonably be expected to make its calculations, assumptions and proposals available in any detailed form to its competitors, there is a need for a central (presumably national) co-ordinating body which can also act as a reservoir of experience in the performance of such analyses. Even if ports improved their pricing systems in social terms, there would still be a need for such a body, for the problem of where to invest would remain. The need would be greatest during the change-over period—it is obvious that all competing ports must change simultaneously, because otherwise there might be massive diversions of cargo and ships to ports with the lowest charges, regardless of the bases used. Moreover, the application of marginal social cost pricing to ports with a changing investment and operating-cost pattern is likely to require continuous and fairly detailed supervision, for, whatever the financial bases of port authorities may be, price discrimination (in the sense of charging different rates for different commodities which impose similar costs) will remain profitable, and port users will doubtless continue to argue that port charges, in whatever form they may be levied, should be as low as possible. It is therefore important that the widespread use of funds retained out of cash surpluses or obtained on fixed interest terms should not be allowed to confuse the situation.

Any discounted cash flow calculation can, of course, contain as many items of uncertainty as there are components of price, cost and output. It therefore contains an ambiguity in the attitude to uncertainty of the entrepreneur concerned. In the approach suggested here this ambiguity remains; there are also two others. First, in spite of the considerable literature on the subject, the proper discount rate for cost-benefit calculations is a matter of some doubt. The social opportunity cost of investment is the net marginal output/capital ratio of the next best alternative project; but if this project is in the private sector there is no very good reason to suppose that this ratio is constant between different projects all of which may be marginal to the private investor. The alternative concept of social time preference can be the subject of interminable argument, none of it, perhaps, founded upon anything very secure.[1] Secondly, there is the problem of the international division of benefits, which depends for its solution upon the long-run elasticities of supply and demand in international seaborne trade. Even to an international aid-administering, or to a supra-national, authority this remains a problem, for it can only be ignored deliberately on the basis of value judgments about the equality of increments of welfare to nations with different populations, different standards of living and different income distributions. Nevertheless, here as elsewhere, decisions cannot be avoided; and if heroic assumptions are required the supply of heroism must be expanded to meet the demand. The application of such ideas as have been described above should, at least, help to avoid mistakes on the scale of those made in the past.

Bearing all this in mind, and particularly the difficulty of sensibly assessing the international division of benefits, it seems all the more important that the pricing system employed by port authorities should be reformed. (At least there is no doubt where the financial benefits of a port investment would lie.) This reformation, therefore, need not achieve perfection—merely a very substantial improvement, and this should not be too difficult to arrange.

[1] See M. S. Feldstein: 'The social time preference discount rate in cost benefit analysis', *Economic Journal*, June 1964.

APPENDIX
PART I

Discounted cash flow may be expressed mathematically as:

$$\text{NPV} = \sum_{i=1}^{i=n} [(R_i - C_i)(1+r)^{-i}] - C_0,$$

where n is the project life from the chosen base year

R_i is the revenue in year i

C_i is the cash cost, including taxes where appropriate, in year i

r is the rate of discount, and

C_0 is the capital cost.

If the capital cost extends, as it may well do, over more than one year, it will itself have to be adjusted to a present value by discounting to the chosen base year (conventionally, but not necessarily, the last year of significant capital expenditure or the last year before any significant revenue accrues) at the same rate of discount as that employed for discounting the rest of the equation. This, of course, involves using values of $(1+r)^{-i}$ in excess of 1, since i then has negative values.

PART II

The arguments presented in the paper may be expressed mathematically as follows:

In the figure $D_i D_i'$ represents the demand curve relating the shadow price (however it may be comprised, and regardless of who is explicitly responsible for paying its various components) of moving a ton of cargo on a given route through the port at which investment is being considered to the cargo tonnage moving in year i. P_1 represents the shadow price and Q_{1i} the cargo tonnage for year i if the investment is not made. P_2 and Q_{2i} represent the same if the investment is made. $P_1 A$, $P_2 BC$, CQ_{2i} and ABQ_{1i} are construction lines parallel to their respective ordinates.

The change in shadow price is therefore $(P_1 - P_2)$ and the diverted and generated cargo flows are $(Q_{2i} - Q_{1i})$. The change in consumers' surplus in respect of the cargo which would flow through this port anyway is thus the diagonally shaded area $P_1 ABP_2 = (P_1 - P_2)Q_{1i}$, and the change in consumers' surplus in respect of the diverted and generated cargo flows is the vertically shaded triangle *ABC*. Since $AB = (P_1 - P_2)$ and $BC = (Q_{2i} - Q_{1i})$ the area

$$ABC = \tfrac{1}{2}(P_1 - P_2)(Q_{2i} - Q_{1i}).$$

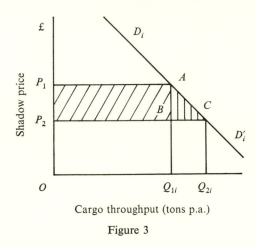

Figure 3

The present value of change in consumers' surplus for year i is therefore $[(P_1 - P_2)Q_{1i} + \tfrac{1}{2}(P_1 - P_2)(Q_{2i} - Q_{1i})](1 + r)^{-i}$ and the present value of the total flow of net benefits to consumers considered thus far is:

$$\sum_{i=1}^{i=n} [(P_1 - P_2)Q_{1i} + \tfrac{1}{2}(P_1 - P_2)(Q_{2i} - Q_{1i})](1 + r)^{-i},$$

where n is again the life of the project. Port investment projects are frequently very long-lived; and at, say, 50 years the discount factor at any credible value of r is so small that it would take a very large rate of growth in consumers' surplus for substantial errors in NPV to be caused by estimating the life of the investment wrongly.[1] In most instances, therefore, no substantial error will be produced by taking $n = 50$, regardless of any probable greater longevity of the project. Instances where n should be taken as less than 50 will usually be fairly obvious, since the relevant value is determined by the physical *or* economic life, whichever is the shorter.

[1] Cf. C. D. Foster and M. E. Beesley, *op. cit.* (1963), p. 50.

The change in the port authority's revenue from dues on ships' tonnage (it has already been argued that this change may be small or even negative) had, so far as it is relevant, been taken into account in calculating the shadow prices. To include it separately would therefore be double counting. The change in dues on cargo (and in any other revenues accruing to the port authority) is represented below by ΔR_{ci}. The time series of the port authority's cash costs (including capital costs) will, of course, also be discounted and is shown here as C_{ci} below. For change in the stock of working capital for year i we may write ΔW_i, regardless of where it is situated or who pays for it. If the project leads to an increase in working capital this will be positive and must (since it is a cost) be subtracted from the other benefits. If it leads to a saving in working capital, then $(W_{2i} - W_{1i})$ will be negative and must be added.

It is unnecessary to discount each of these time series separately. For each year a net figure of:

$$(P_1 - P_2)Q_{1i} + \tfrac{1}{2}(P_1 - P_2)(Q_{2i} - Q_{1i}) + (\Delta R_{ci} - \Delta C_{ci}) - \Delta W_i$$

may be calculated for each trade route concerned and discounted to the base year. The full formula, therefore, is:

$$\text{NPV} = \sum_{i=1}^{i=n} [(P_1 - P_2)Q_{1i} + (P_2 - P_2)\tfrac{1}{2}(Q_{2i} - Q_{1i})$$
$$+ (\Delta R_{ci} - \Delta C_{ci}) - \Delta W_i](1+r)^{-i}.$$

But this assumes either that the whole of the consumers' surplus remains within the investing country or that its international distribution is of no consequence. It also assumes that the whole of the change in working capital benefits (or, if it is an increase, is a charge on) the investing country. If we write S_{Ri} for the proportion of consumers' surplus assumed to remain within the investing country in year i, and P for the proportion of the change in working capital which benefits (or is a charge on) the investing country, the formula becomes:

$$\text{NPV} = \sum_{i=0}^{i=n} [(P_1 - P_2)Q_{1i}S_R + \tfrac{1}{2}(P_1 - P_2)S_R(Q_{2i} - Q_{1i})$$
$$+ (\Delta R_{ci} - \Delta C_{ci}) - P\Delta W_i](1+r)^{-i}$$

and we may follow the investment rules of accepting all (except mutually exclusive) projects with positive net present values and choosing among mutually exclusive projects (e.g. different depths, quay lengths, numbers of cranes or starting dates) by selecting the one with the greatest NPV.[1]

[1] Except under capital rationing. Then, and only then, does the ratio of NPV to capital cost indicate the best project. This should not be confused with cost-benefit ratios as usually understood, i.e. with ratios of average or total discounted benefits to average or total discounted costs. A further exception to the rule of maximizing NPV is that of mutually exclusive projects with different lives. The rule is then to accept the project whose NPV is equivalent to the greatest annuity obtainable, at the same discount rate, over the life of the particular project concerned. Decisions between mutually exclusive projects, including those with different lives, may also be made by calculating the incremental or differential rates of return. On this last point see, e.g. Merrett and Sykes: *op. cit* (p. 158).

INDEX

accuracy, spurious, 7, 85

aesthetics: in seaports, *see* intangibles; in ship designs, 81

air transport, 1, 18

airports, 8

Alexander Report, 14 n., 25

Alfred, A. M., 73 n., 77, 164 n.

American President Lines, 36

Anderson, J., 63 n.

annuities: formula, 137; tables, 108, 137; use of, with differential project lives, 83

anomalies: (*see also* extended yield); in calculating internal rates of return, 85–6

anti-fouling paint, perpetual, 75

Anti-Trust Acts (of USA) and shipping conferences, 23, 25, 27, 29, 30, 36, 41; (*see also* USA legislation)

Argyriadis, D. A., 155 n.

Attwood, E. L., 63 n.

Australia: crew costs in, 60; and shipping conferences, 45

automatic helmsman, 100

automation: defined, 100; examples of, 100; economic effects of, 101–2; in British shipping, 6–7, **100–31**

average total cost *see* marginal costs; shadow prices

backhaul effect *see* tramps, unbalanced trades

Baker, G. S., 63 n., 64, 89 n.

'Baker–Tutin–Kent formula', 64, 73, 88–9; criticized, 65–6

balance of payments effects and shipping: analysis of, 3, **46–60**; and capital costs, 51–3; and common assertions on, 46, 54–5; and compared with other industries, 53, 54–5; and crews' wages, 50 53, 60; in cross-trades, 47, 48, 49, 50, 54; and currency convertibility, 48; and discriminatory controls, 48, 51; and exaggeration of, 54; and finance, 54, 57–60; and location of expenditure, 49–52; and management costs, 50–1; and newly-generated income, 49; and profitability, 53, 54; and second-hand ships, 52–3; and ship costs, 49–51, 55–60; and ship designs, 66–7; and speech by Admiral Harlee, 44; and worked examples of, 58–60

balancing charge, 94, 104

Baltic and International Maritime Conference, 4 n.

Barnaby, K. C., 62 n.

base-year, the choice of, 80, 170

Beesley, Professor M. E., 73 n., 82 n., 152 n., 162 n., 172 n., 174 n., 184 n.

Benford, Professor H. 5, 6, 63 n., 84, 153 n., 176–8

Bergius, W. C., 63 n.

Bes, J., 163 n.

Bierman, H., 73 n.

Biles, Professor Sir J. H., 63 n., 159 n.

Bird, Dr J., 157 n.

Bonner Act (PL 87–346), 2, **22–3**, **25–45**: administration of, 33–35; avoidance of, 35, 42; and conference agreements, 33, 35–7; and disclosure of information, 33; and discriminatory agreements, 36; and discriminatory freight rates, 33; and dual rates, 28, 30–2; effective date of, 25; failure of, 42–3; one-sidedness of, 23, 37; predecessor 25; purposes of, 28, 41–3; and self-policing, 32–3, 37–41; and tariff-filing, 33; vagueness of, 23, 36–7, 38, 42

Bonner Committee, 29

Bonner Report, 14, 25

Bonner, Representative, 28, 34, 40, 42

British Iron and Steel Research Association, 157 n.

British Ship Research Association, 7 n.

broken stowage, allowances for, 134

bulk cargoes, 13, 152 (*see also* bulk carriers)

[187]

bulk carriers (dry), 9, 10, 13, 168, 175, 177
Buxton, Dr I. L., 7 n.

Cabotage, 13, 28, 48
Campbell, F. S. Capt., 157 n.
capital, charges, 133 (*see also* depreciation); cost, after allowing for investment grant, 107; costs, in the balance of payments, 51–3; costs in the optimization of ship designs, 68–9; costs and contract prices, 69; costs, treatment in d.c.f. 70; equity, 53; fixed-interest, 7, 52, 53, 74, 77, 78, 165 181; -intensity of shipping, 166–7; productivity of, 71; rationing, 6, 186; recovery factor, 5, 177; utilization, 136
cargo liners, *see* liners, cargo
cargo-handling; advanced techniques of, 9, 151, 153; costs, 7, 19, 153; rates, in tons per gross port day, 142; and shadow prices, 7, 168
catering department, effects of crew savings on, 102
Cayzer, Sir Nicholas, 133 n.; 147 n.
Celler Committee, 29, 39, 41; Report, 14 n., 29, 32; Representative, 40
Ceylon, 11
Chamber of Shipping of UK, 20 n.
Channel Tunnel, 81
Chapman, L. B., 63 n.
Chapman, R., 157 n.
charters, long-term in d.c.f. 74; rates, 163 (*see also* freight rates); to supplement liner services, 26; types of, 13, 163
Church, J. E., 63 n.
Civil Engineers, Institution of, 9
classification societies *see* surveys
Coburn, T. M., 82 n., 162 n., 174 n.
Committee of American Steamship
compound interest, 71
Lines, 28 n.
conferences, shipping: closed, 18, 26, 27; competition with, 17, 27, 139, 171; complaints concerning, 15, 20–21; conclusion of UNCTAD on, 15; co-ordination in, 17; defined, 14; elasticity of supply in, 26; European Ministers of Transport, support of,

20–2; 'formula system' in, 21–2; freight rates in, 1, **10–12**, **15–22**, **26–45**; minutes, and FMC, 41; negotiations with shippers, 20–2; open, 18, 26; and port authorities, 11; and port congestion, 26; and port surcharges, 26; profits in, 17–18, 21–2, 27; self-policing, and FMC, 32–3; structure of rates in, 19, 34–5; supported by shippers, 15, 17, 29; tariffs, 15, 19; USA regulation of, **22–4**, **24–45**
conflicts of jurisdiction (*see* national jurisdiction)
congestion costs, 160, 179–180
Congressional Information Bureau, 25 n.
'conservancy' functions, 160
Constitution (of USA), Fifth Amendment to, 40
Consumers' Association, the, 77
consumers' surplus, 170; calculation of, 183–6; international division of, 172–4, 185–6
container(s): berths, 3, 155–6; comparisons with conventional ships, 151, conditions for success, 3, 155; cost of, 150; cranes, 154; and packing costs, 165; and pilferage, 165; revolutionary nature of, 1, 154–6; services, 150, 154, 156; ships, 155–6, 175, 178; stowage of, in conventional ships, 155; USA regulation of, 2–3
correctibility, of currencies, 48
Cooper, L. K., 25 n.
Corlett, Dr E. C. B., 63 n.
cost-benefit-analysis, and d.c.f., 161–2; in Channel Tunnel, 82; in London–Birmingham motorway, 82; in ports, 8, **161–186**; in public service craft, 81–2
cost-benefit ratios, 162
costs: capital, *see* capital costs; in cargo liners, 55–9, 132–6; in d.c.f. 68–9; of major maritime powers, 55; overhead, 19, 87; per ton mile, 141; reduction of, 9; of sea transport, 9 (*see also* shadow prices)
Councils, Shippers', 20–1
Crake, R. T., 64 n., 154 n., 156
Cufley, C. F. H., 14 n.

data-logger, 100
Day, J. V., 44
'deducted spaces', 158
deepening of ports and harbours, 153,
156, 158, 159, 160, 166
deferred rebates: allowed to USA shipowners in other trades, 36; defined
and described, 14–15, 26; limitations
of 17–19; prohibited in USA trades, 25
depreciation, 57, 60, 69, 87, 133, 177;
allowance for tax purposes, 93,
104–6; and double-counting, 69, 138;
free, 105–6, 111–2, 113, 125, 167;
replacement, 161
Dept. of Applied Economics, Cambridge, 2 n.
Dept. of Justice (of USA), (*see also*
Anti-Trust Acts) 27, 30, 37;
Dept. of State (of USA), 30, 162 n.
Dept. of Transportation (of USA), 2
Devlin Report, 8
diesel engines, 56, 132, 177
differential yield *see* incremental yield.
discontinuities in ship design, 65
discounted cash flow (d.c.f.): calculation time, 101; complexity of, 5–6;
and cost-benefit analysis, 161; and
discounted costs, 158; and optimal
prices, 161; and optimizing ports,
158–61; and optimizing ship designs,
5, **68–88**; short-cut methods, 126;
worked examples of, 90–9, 121–6
discount factors: and capital recovery
factor, 177; derivation of, 71; use of,
in d.c.f., 71–2, 103
discounting the future, 70–1
discount rate: for balance of payments
effects, 55; for cost-benefit analysis,
178, 182; for d.c.f., 76–8, 135;
raising, for uncertainty 79, 166–7; and
sensitivity of shadow prices, 140
discrimination: in cargo liner freight
rates, 10–11, 19; in port charges, 160,
181
distribution of profits to shareholders,
105
diversion of cargo, 158, 159, 169–70,
171, 173, 176
Dorfman, R., 165 n.
Doust, Dr D. J., 64 n.
dredgers, design of, 81–2

dredging *see* deepening of ports and
harbours and reclamation
dual rates (dual-rate contracts): defined
and described, 14–15, 26, 28; legalisa-
tion of, 28–9, 30–2, 41, 42, 43,
limitations of, 17–19
Dupuit, J., 161

economics, elementary textbooks of, 68
economic welfare, 67
economies of ship size, 10, 152
Eddison, R. T., 157 n.
effective consumer of sea transport, 172
elasticity of demand for sea transport,
16–18, 168, 169–70, 173–4, 183–4
Elden, R. M., 63 n., 69
end-year cash flows, the choice of, 80
(*see also* mid-year cash flows)
Engineers, Civil, *see* Civil Engineers,
Institution of
entrepôt trade, 172
equivalent interest rate of return, *see*
internal rate of return
European Ministers of Transport:
meetings of, 20; statement by, 20
'exempted spaces', 158
exports: of USA theories of government, 40; freight rates on, and
balance of payments, 48; elasticity
of demand for, 173
extended yield method: described,
85–6; used in example, 97

factors of production: defined, 67;
necessary assumption of homo-
geneity, 67; (*see also* productivity)
Fairplay, 57 n.
Federal Courts of Appeal, (of USA),
39
Federal Maritime Board (of USA), 27,
29, 30, 43
Staff, 34
'all agreements' order, 1960, 39
Federal Maritime Commission, 2, 23,
27–45; (*see also* USA Legislation and
conferences, shipping), alleged bias
of, 43–4; appeals from, 39; budget,
34; compromises with, 40; and conference agreements, 32–3, 35–7;
curious views on discrimination,
34–5; delays by, 37; domination by